W9-BBC-285

Library/Media Center
Carroll Community College
1601 Washington Road
Westminster, Maryland 21157

WITHDRAWN

Modern Critical Views

Modern Critical Views

Modern Critical Views

SYLVIA PLATH

Edited and with an introduction by
Harold Bloom
Sterling Professor of the Humanities
Yale University

CHELSEA HOUSE PUBLISHERS
New York ◇ Philadelphia

© 1989 by Chelsea House Publishers, a division
of Main Line Book Co.

Introduction © 1988 by Harold Bloom

All rights reserved. No part of this publication may be
reproduced or transmitted in any form or by any means
without the written permission of the publisher.

Printed and bound in the United States of America

10   9   8   7   6   5   4

∞ The paper used in this publication meets the minimum
requirements of the American National Standard for Permanence
of Paper for Printed Library Materials, Z39.48–1984.

Library of Congress Cataloging in Publication Data
Sylvia Plath.
    (Modern critical views)
    Bibliography: p.
    Includes index.
    1. Plath, Sylvia—Criticism and interpretation.
I. Bloom, Harold.   II. Series.
PS3566.L27Z914   1988   811'.54   87–25677
ISBN 1–55546–280–4

Contents

Editor's Note

This book brings together a representative selection of the best criticism available on the writings of Sylvia Plath. The critical essays are reprinted here in the chronological sequence of their original publication. I am grateful to Susanna Gilbert for her assistance in editing this volume.

My introduction, rather sadly, is a negative report as to my rereading of Plath's most famous poems, since they seem of a sort that I am not yet competent to judge. Irving Howe begins the chronological sequence of criticism with his own dissent from the Plath admirers, though he grants her "a gift for the single, isolate image," and I myself cannot locate any such images of poetic value.

Comparing Plath to Dylan Thomas, D. F. McKay sees her energies as "invoking the absent afflatus," while Thomas both defends himself against and yearns to join a supposedly primal force. Plath's only novel, *The Bell Jar,* is analyzed by Stan Smith as leaving unresolved tensions between authentic self-articulation and public or ritual image.

The distinguished feminist critic Sandra M. Gilbert writes a poignant appreciation of her attachment to Plath's works. Hugh Kenner, most distinguished of High Modernist critics, expresses admiration for the promise of *The Colossus,* but confesses sadness at the "bogus spirituality" of *Ariel.* In a generous overview, J. D. McClatchy concludes that Plath's "consistency and importance lie in her experiments with voice," while Mary Lynn Broe reads the six poems of the bee sequence as a work where "the triumphal energy of performance coexists with a small constructiveness and counseled limitations."

Ted Hughes, British Poet Laureate, once Plath's husband, describes her journal as the witness of "her real creation," the "eventual birth of a new self-conquering self." We return to *The Bell Jar* with Lynda K. Bundtzen's account of self-victimization in that novel. "Lady Lazarus," the famous poem that I fail to admire in my introduction, is traced through its manuscript

development by Susan Van Dyne, who regards the poem as "monumental."
Melody Zajdel then concludes this volume with a consideration of Plath's
short stories, which she judges as well-wrought preparations for the "haunting powerful craftsmanship" of *The Bell Jar*.

Introduction

When I was much younger, I believed firmly that critics should not write about poetry that they did not love, indeed had not loved for a long time. I met and liked Sylvia Plath a third of a century ago in Cambridge, England, and remember then reading her earliest poems with respectful interest. Purchasing *The Colossus* in 1960, I expected a touch more than I received, and found the volume too derivative, though accomplished enough. Plath killed herself in 1963, and *Ariel* was published in 1965. I shied away from the book and did not purchase and read it until the early 1970s. Perhaps I would have liked it better then, or could now, if its few merits were not so grossly exaggerated by its many admirers. Perhaps not.

Plath was not Christina Rossetti or even Elizabeth Barrett Browning. If we compare her to an original and powerful poet of her own generation, like the superb May Swenson, then she quite dwindles away. Contemporary reputation is a most inadequate guide to canonical survival. The more fanciful of Plath's admirers have ventured to link her to Emily Dickinson, the most original consciousness and most formidable intellect among all poets in the language since William Blake. A far better comparison would be to Mrs. Felicia Hemans, English Romantic versifier, whose tragic early death gave her a certain glamour for a time. Mrs. Hemans is remembered today solely for her dramatic lyric, "Casabianca," with its abrupt opening line, "The boy stood on the burning deck," most memorably parodied by the wag who completed the couplet with: "Eating peanuts by the peck." "Lady Lazarus" is the "Casabianca" of my generation and may endure, as such, in some future edition of that marvelous anthology *The Stuffed Owl*.

I do not intend to be contentious, and I have been preceded in my reservations by two critics who are very different both from one another and from myself, Irving Howe and Hugh Kenner. Dr. Samuel Johnson, the Sublime of criticism, took on his *Lives of the English Poets* with the understanding that the choice of poets was to be that of the booksellers, whose

1

object was to satisfy the taste of the time. In that spirit, Johnson cheerfully
suggested the inclusion of such mighty pens as Yalden and Pomfret to join
such eminent hands as Stepney, Sprat, Tickell, Mallet, and Lyttleton. The
fashions of each moment in literary history are not unlike each moment in
sartorial tradition. Sprat went the way of the bustle. Hysterical intensity,
whatever its momentary erotic appeal, is not an affect that endures in verse.
Poetry relies upon trope and not upon sincerity. I have just reread *Ariel,* after
some fifteen years, and spontaneously I find myself again murmuring Oscar
Wilde's definitive apothegm: "All bad poetry springs from genuine feeling."
There are the immensely celebrated pieces, including "Lady Lazarus" with
its much-admired conclusion:

> Dying
> Is an art, like everything else.
> I do it exceptionally well.
>
> I do it so it feels like hell.
> I do it so it feels real.
> I guess you could say I've a call.
>
> It's easy enough to do it in a cell.
> It's easy enough to do it and stay put.
> It's the theatrical
>
> Comeback in broad day
> To the same place, the same face, the same brute
> Amused shout:
>
> "A miracle!"
> That knocks me out.
> There is a charge
>
> For the eyeing of my scars, there is a charge
> For the hearing of my heart—
> It really goes.
>
> And there is a charge, a very large charge
> For a word or a touch
> Or a bit of blood
>
> Or a piece of my hair or my clothes.
> So, so, Herr Doktor.
> So, Herr Enemy.

I am your opus,
I am your valuable,
The pure gold baby

That melts to a shriek.
I turn and burn.
Do not think I underestimate your great concern.

Ash, ash—
You poke and stir.
Flesh, bone, there is nothing there—

A cake of soap,
A wedding ring,
A gold filling.

Herr God, Herr Lucifer
Beware
Beware.

Out of the ash
I rise with my red hair
And I eat men like air.

Helen Vendler calls this "a tantrum of style" and "a centrifugal spin to further and further reaches of outrage." Those seem to me characteristically kind judgments from a severe student of poetic syntax, the most authoritative in my critical generation. I become lost, and doubt my competence to read Plath (or Adrienne Rich and other seers of the School of Resentment), when I encounter feminist defenses of Plath's final mode, as here in Mary Lynn Broe:

> We lack a critical vocabulary for these rich tones. We lack a critical vocabulary precisely because our society lacks any definition of power which *transforms* rather than *coerces*.

This is to tell me, presumably, that I can write criticism of Emily Dickinson, Elizabeth Bishop, and May Swenson because they manifest a power of *coercion* while Plath, Rich, Alice Walker defeat me because I do not know how to describe and analyze a power of *transformation*. "Lady Lazarus," with its gratuitous and humanly offensive appropriation of the imagery of Jewish martyrs in Nazi death camps (an appropriation incessant in Plath) seems to me a pure instance of coercive rhetoric, transforming absolutely nothing. That the reader is harangued, not persuaded, is my baffled protest. Barbara Hardy, however, hears an "unfailing grim humor" and a "rationally alert intelligence" in "Lady Lazarus" and its companion poems:

> It is present in the great *Ariel* poems: "Lady Lazarus," "Daddy," "Death & Co.," "A Birthday Present," and "The Applicant," which are very outgoing, very deranged, very enlarged. In "Lady Lazarus" the persona is split, and deranged. The split allows the poem to peel off the personal, to impersonate suicidal feeling and generalize it. It is a skill, it is a show, something to look at. The poem seems to be admitting the exhibitionism of suicide (and death poetry?) as well as the voyeurism of spectators (and readers?). It is also a foul resurrection, stinking of death. This image allows her to horrify us, to complain of being revived, to attack God and confuse him with a doctor, any doctor (bringing round a suicide) and a Doktor in a concentration camp, experimenting in life and death. It moves from Herr Doktor to Herr Enemy and to miracle makers, scientists, the torturer who may be a scientist, to Christ, Herr God, and Herr Lucifer (the last two after all collaborated in experiments on Adam, Eve, and Job). They poke and nose around in the ashes, and this is the last indignity, forcing the final threat: "I eat men like air." It is a threat that can intelligibly be made by martyred victims (she has red hair, is Jewish), by phoenixes, by fire, by women. The fusion and dispersal, once more rational and irrational, makes the pattern of controlled derangement, creating not one mirror but a hall of mirrors, all differently distorting, and revealing many horrors.

The poem "Lady Lazarus," here as elsewhere, provokes a mode of criticism that Plath herself deeply contaminates. I have no desire to invoke "The Fallacy of Imitative Form," a legacy of the critic Yvor Winters. Plath's fate was poignant; whether "Lady Lazarus" is poignant, or a tantrum, or even a poignant tantrum, seems to me an aesthetic question to which a clear answer indeed can be made. If Plath's achievement (and Rich's) is indeed so original and so great that it calls for a new aesthetic, then let that aesthetic come down upon us. Until the aesthetic of Resentment has achieved itself, the later poetry of Sylvia Plath will abide with its admirers.

IRVING HOWE

The Plath Celebration:
A Partial Dissent

A glamour of fatality hangs over the name of Sylvia Plath, the glamour that has made her a darling of our culture. Extremely gifted, her will clenched into a fist of ambition, several times driven to suicide by a suffering so absolute as to seem almost impersonal, yet in her last months composing poems in which pathology and clairvoyance triumphantly fuse—these are the materials of her legend. It is a legend that solicits our desires for a heroism of sickness that can serve as emblem of the age, and many young readers take in Sylvia Plath's vibrations of despair as if they were the soul's own oxygen. For reasons good and bad, the spokesmen for the sensibility of extreme gesture—all the blackness, confession, denial, and laceration that are warranted by modern experience but are also the moral bromides of our moment—see in Sylvia Plath an authentic priestess. Because she is authentic, the role would surely displease her; dead now for a decade, she can offer no defense.

Quantities of adoring criticism pile up around her, composed in a semi-mimetic frenzy designed to be equivalent in tone to its subject. The result is poor criticism, worse prose. In a collection of essays devoted to Sylvia Plath, the editor writes—almost as if he too were tempted by an oven: "The courting of experience that kills is characteristic of major poets" (*The Art of Sylvia Plath,* ed. Charles Newman). Is it? Virgil, Petrarch, Goethe, Pope, Hugo, Wordsworth, Bialik, Yeats, Stevens, Auden, Frost?

In dissenting a little from the Plath celebration, one has the sense not so much of disagreeing about the merits of certain poems as of plunging into

From *The Critical Point of Literature and Culture.* © 1973 by Irving Howe. Horizon Press, 1973.

a harsh *kulturkampf*. For one party in this struggle Sylvia Plath has become an icon, and the dangers for those in the other party are also considerable, since it would be unjust to allow one's irritation with her devotees to spill over into one's response to her work. So let us move quickly to the facts about her career and then to the poems she wrote toward the end of her life, crucial for any judgment of her work.

Her father, a professor of biology and (it's important to note) a man of German descent, died when she was nine. The reverberations of this event are heavy in the poems, though its precise significance for Sylvia Plath as either person or poet is very hard to grasp. She then lived with her mother in Wellesley, Massachusetts; she went to Smith, an ardent student who swept up all the prizes; she suffered from psychic disorders; she won a Fullbright to Cambridge University, then met and married a gifted English poet, Ted Hughes. In 1960 she published her first book of poems, *The Colossus*—it rings with distinguished echoes, proclaims unripe gifts, contains more quotable passages than successful poems (true for all her work). She had two children, in 1960 and 1962, to whom she seems to have been fiercely attached and about whom she wrote some of her better poems. She was separated from her husband, lived one freezing winter in London with her children, and, experiencing an onslaught of energy at once overwhelming and frightening, wrote her best-known poems during the last weeks of her life. On February 11, 1963, she killed herself.

Crossing the Water contains some of the poems she wrote between the early work of *The Colossus* and the final outburst that would appear posthumously in 1965 as *Ariel*. There are graphic lines in *Crossing the Water*, but few poems fully achieved. "The desert is white as a blind man's eye, / Comfortless as salt" we read in a poem not otherwise notable. The drive to self-destruction that would tyrannize the last poems is already at work in these "middle" ones:

> If I pay the roots of the heather
> Too close attention, they will invite me
> To whiten my bones among them.

The poems in *Crossing the Water* are, nevertheless, more open in voice and variable in theme than those for which Sylvia Plath has become famous; they have less power but also less pathology. She writes well, in snatches and stanzas, about the impersonal moments of personal experience, when the sense of everything beyond one's selfhood dominates the mind. She writes well, that is, precisely about the portion of human experience that is most absent in the *Ariel* poems; such poems as "Parliament Hill Fields," "Small

Hours," and a few others in *Crossing the Water,* unheroic in temper and unforced in pitch, can yield familiar pleasures. The flaws in her work she describes charmingly in "Stillborn," though it's characteristic that, after the vivid opening stanza, the poem should itself seem stillborn:

> These poems do not live: it's a sad diagnosis.
> They grew their toes and fingers well enough,
> Their little foreheads bulged with concentration.
> If they missed out on walking about like people
> It wasn't for any lack of mother love.

II

At a crucial point in her career Sylvia Plath came under the influence of Robert Lowell's *Life Studies,* and it is this relationship that has led many admirers to speak of her late work as "confessional poetry." The category is interesting but dubious, both in general and when applied to Sylvia Plath.

In *Life Studies* Lowell broke into a new style. He abandoned the complex interlacings of idea and image, the metaphysical notations and ironic turnings of his earlier work, and instead wrote poems that were to deal immediately with his own experience: his time as CO, his nervous breakdowns, his relations with his wife. When he wrote "I" it was clear he really did mean his private self, not a *persona* created for the poem's occasion. To the small number of people who read poetry at all, *Life Studies* came as a valued, perhaps overvalued, shock—a harsh abandonment of the Eliotian impersonality that had previously dominated American poetry. Inevitably, this new style was widely imitated and its inherent difficulty frequently ignored. The readiness with which Lowell exposed his own life caused people to admire his courage rather than scrutinize his poems. Candor was raised to an absolute value, such as it need not often be in either morals or literature. Our culture was then starting to place an enormous stress on self-exposure, self-assault, self-revelation—as if spontaneity were a sure warrant of authenticity, and spilling out a sure road to comprehension. The bared breast replaced the active head.

Insofar as a poem depends mainly on the substance of its confession, as blow or shock revealing some hidden shame in the writer's experience, it will rarely be a first-rate piece of work. It will lack the final composure that even the most excited composition requires. Insofar as it makes the confessional element into something integral to the poem, it ceases, to that extent, to be confessional. It becomes a self-sufficient poem, not dependent for its value on whatever experience may have evoked it. Perhaps the greatest

achievement of this kind in English is the group of poems Thomas Hardy
wrote in 1912–13 after the death of his first wife: they are full of the regrets
of wasted life, missed opportunities, shamed quarrels, but they take on an
autonomous life, beyond the rawness of confession.

Now, this is dogma and, as such, suspect—even by those who may agree
with it. For obviously there are cases where residues of personal confession
can be detected, yet the poem constitutes more than a mere notation of
incident or memory. I would also add that the short lyric is a form likely to
resist confessional writing, since it does not allow for the sustained moral
complication, the full design of social or historical setting, that can transform
confession from local act to larger meaning. The confessions of Augustine
and Rousseau are long works, and they are in prose.

A flaw in confessional poetry, even the best of it, is one that character-
izes much other American poetry in the twentieth century. It is the notion
that a careful behavioral notation of an event or object is in itself sufficient
basis for composing a satisfactory poem: the description of an orange, a
wheelbarrow, a woman's gait. What such poems depend on, for their very
life, is the hope of creating an aura, a network of implication, that will
enlarge the scope of their references. Sometimes, as in Frost's "Spring Pools,"
this feat is managed; too often, what we get is a mere verbal snapshot, a
discrete instance, that has little reverberation. And this holds true even if the
snapshot records an event that rouses our curiosity or dismay.

Robert Lowell's poem, "Man and Wife," shook many readers when it
first appeared in 1952. When you read a poem that begins—

> Tamed by Miltown, we lie on Mother's bed;
> the rising sun in war paint dyes us red;
> in broad daylight her gilded bedposts shine,
> abandoned, almost Dionysian.

—some feeling of involvement, even pain, is likely to be invoked through the
very announcement of its subject. There is the compressed suggestibility of
"Mother's bed," the vividness of the "war paint" in the second line. But the
poem as a whole no longer seems quite so remarkable as I once thought. In
the middle—and the middle is where confessional poems get into trouble,
once the subject has been declared and something must now be *done* with
it—Lowell declines into a recollection about the time he "outdrank the Rahvs
in the heat / Of Greenwich Village." Most readers do not know "the Rahvs,"
and the reference is therefore lost upon them; those few who do may find it
possible to resist the poet's intention. Here the poem has slipped into self-
indulgence. At the end, Lowell does achieve a recovery with several lines

describing his wife's invective after a quarrel, presumably before Miltown "tamed" them both:

> your old-fashioned tirade—
> loving, rapid, merciless—
> breaks like the Atlantic Ocean on my head.

These lines move the center of the poem away from the confessing, preening self of the poet and reveal a counteraction: that's not just a prop lying there in bed with him, it's another human being. True, the reference remains local and thereby, perhaps, open to the kind of criticism I made earlier of confessional poetry as a whole. But through severe detail Lowell has managed to suggest reverberations that move the poem beyond the edges of his personal wound.

At times Sylvia Plath also wrote confessional poetry, as in the much-praised "Lady Lazarus," a poem about her recurrent suicide attempts. Its opening lines, like almost all her opening lines, come at one like a driven hammer:

> I have done it again.
> One year in every ten
> I manage it—
>
> A sort of walking miracle, my skin
> Bright as a Nazi lampshade,
> My right foot
>
> A paperweight,
> My face a featureless, fine
> Jew linen.

The tone is jeeringly tough, but at least partly directed against herself. There is a strain of self-irony ("a sort of walking miracle") such as poetry of this kind can never have enough of. Still, one must be infatuated with the Plath legend to ignore the poet's need for enlarging the magnitude of her act through illegitimate comparisons with the Holocaust (a point to which I will return later).

Sylvia Plath's most notable gift as a writer—a gift for the single, isolate image—comes through later in the poem when, recalling an earlier suicide attempt, she writes that they had to "pick the worms off me like sticky pearls." But then, after patching together some fragments of recollection, she collapses into an archness about her suicide attempts that is shocking in a way she could not have intended:

I do it so it feels like hell.
I do it so it feels real.
I guess you could say I've a call.

It's easy enough to do it in a cell,
It's easy enough to do it and stay put.

As if uneasy about the tone of such lines, she then drives toward what I can only see as a willed hysteric tone, the forcing of language to make up for an inability to develop the matter. The result is sentimental violence:

A cake of soap,
A wedding ring,
A gold filling.
.   .   .   .   .
Out of the ash
I rise with my red hair
And I eat men like air.

In the end, the several remarkable lines in this poem serve only to intensify its badness, for in their isolation, without the support of a rational structure, they leave the author with no possibility of development other than violent wrenchings in tone. And this is a kind of badness that seems a constant temptation in confessional poetry, the temptation to reveal all with one eye nervously measuring the effect of revelation.

There's another famous poem by Sylvia Plath entitled "Cut" in which she shows the same mixture of strong phrasing and structural incoherence. "Cut" opens on a sensational note, or touch:

What a thrill—
My thumb instead of an onion.
The top quite gone
Except for a sort of hinge

Of skin,
A flap like a hat,
Dead white.
Then that red plush.

This is vivid, no denying it. Morbid too. The question is whether the morbidity is an experience the writer struggles with or yields to, examines dispassionately or caresses indulgently.

There is a saving wit in the opening lines ("My thumb instead of an onion") and this provides some necessary distance between invoked experience and invoking speaker. But the poem collapses through Sylvia Plath's inability to do more with her theme than thrust it against our eyes, displaying her wound in all its red plushy woundedness.

> The stain on your
> Gauze Ku Klux Klan
> Babushka
> Darkens and tarnishes.

The bandage is seen as a babushka, an old lady's scarf. All right. But the Ku Klux Klan? And still more dubious, the "Ku Klux Klan Babushka?" One supposes the KKK is being used here because it is whitely repressive, the Babushka-bandage is "repressing" the blood, and in the poem's graphic pathology, the flow of blood from the cut is attractive, fruitful, perhaps healthy ("a celebration, this is," runs one line). But even if my reading is accurate, does that help us very much with the stanza? Isn't it an example of weakness through excess?

Sylvia Plath's most famous poem, adored by many sons and daughters, is "Daddy." It is a poem with an affecting theme, the feelings of the speaker as she regathers the pain of her father's premature death and her persuasion that he has betrayed her by dying:

> I was ten when they buried you.
> At twenty I tried to die
> And get back, back, back to you.

In the poem Sylvia Plath identifies the father (we recall his German birth) with the Nazis ("Panzer-man, panzer-man, O You") and flares out with assaults for which nothing in the poem (nor, so far as we know, in Sylvia Plath's own life) offers any warrant: "A cleft in your chin instead of your foot / But no less a devil for that." Nor does anything in the poem offer warrant, other than the free-flowing hysteria of the speaker, for the assault of such lines as "There's a stake in your fat black heart / And the villagers never liked you." Or for the snappy violence of

> Every woman adores a Fascist,
> The boot in the face, the brute
> Brute heart of a brute like you.

What we have here is a revenge fantasy, feeding upon filial love-hatred, and thereby mostly of clinical interest. But seemingly aware that the merely clinical can't provide the materials for a satisfying poem, Sylvia Plath tries

to enlarge upon the personal plight, give meaning to the personal outcry, by
fancying the girl as victim of a Nazi father:

> An engine, an engine
> Chuffing me off like a Jew.
> A Jew to Dachau, Auschwitz, Belsen.
> I began to talk like a Jew,
> I think I may well be a Jew.

The more sophisticated admirers of this poem may say that I fail to see
it as a dramatic presentation, a monologue spoken by a disturbed girl not
necessarily to be identified with Sylvia Plath, despite the similarities of detail
between the events of the poem and the events of her life. I cannot accept
this view. The personal-confessional element, strident and undisciplined, is
simply too obtrusive to suppose the poem no more than a dramatic picture
of a certain style of disturbance. If, however, we did accept such a reading of "Daddy," we would fatally narrow its claims to emotional or moral
significance, for we would be confining it to a mere vivid imagining of a
pathological state. That, surely, is not how its admirers really take the poem.

It is clearly not how the critic George Steiner takes the poem when he
calls it "the 'Guernica' of modern poetry." But then, in an astonishing turn,
he asks: "In what sense does anyone, himself uninvolved and long after the
event, commit a subtle larceny when he invokes the echoes and trappings
of Auschwitz and appropriates an enormity of ready emotion to his own
private design?" The question is devastating to his early comparison with
"Guernica." Picasso's painting objectifies the horrors of Guernica, through
the distancing of art; no one can suppose that he shares or participates in
them. Plath's poem aggrandizes on the "enormity of ready emotion" invoked
by references to the concentration camps, in behalf of an ill-controlled if
occasionally brilliant outburst. There is something monstrous, utterly dis-
proportionate, when tangled emotions about one's father are deliberately
compared with the historical fate of the European Jews; something sad, if the
comparison is made spontaneously. "Daddy" persuades one again, through
the force of negative example, of how accurate T. S. Eliot was in saying,
"The more perfect the artist, the more completely separate in him will be the
man who suffers and the mind which creates."

III

The most interesting poems in *Ariel* are not confessional at all. A confessional poem would seem to be one in which the writer speaks *to* the reader,

telling him, without the mediating presence of imagined event or *persona*, something about his life: I had a nervous breakdown, my wife and I sometimes lie in bed, sterile of heart, through sterile nights. The sense of direct speech addressed to an audience is central to confessional writing. But the most striking poems Sylvia Plath wrote are quite different. They are poems written out of an extreme condition, a state of being in which the speaker, for all practical purposes Sylvia Plath herself, has abandoned the sense of audience and cares nothing about—indeed, is hardly aware of—the presence of anyone but herself. She writes with a hallucinatory, self-contained fervor. She addresses herself to the air, to the walls. She speaks not as a daylight self, with its familiar internal struggles and doubts, its familiar hesitations before the needs and pressures of others. There is something utterly monolithic, fixated about the voice that emerges in these poems, a voice unmodulated and asocial.

It's as if we are overhearing the rasps of a mind that has found its own habitation and need not measure its distance from, even consider its relation to, other minds. And the stakes are far higher than can ever be involved in mere confession. She exists in some mediate province between living and dying, and she appears to be balancing coolly the claims of the two, drawn almost equally to both yet oddly comfortable with the perils of where she is. This is not the by-now worn romanticism of *Liebestod*. It is something very strange, very fearful: a different kind of existence, at ease at the gate of dying. The poems Sylvia Plath wrote in this state of being are not "great" poems, but one can hardly doubt that they are remarkable. For they do bring into poetry an element of experience that, so far as I know, is new, and thereby they advance the thrust of literary modernism by another inch or so. A poem like "Kindness" is set squarely in what I have called the mediate province between living and dying:

> What is so real as the cry of a child?
> A rabbit's cry may be wilder
> But it has no soul.

And then, a few lines later:

> The blood jet is poetry,
> There is no stopping it.

The poems written out of this strange equilibrium—"Fever 103°," "Totem," "Edge"—are notable, and the best of them seems to me "Edge":

> The woman is perfected.
> Her dead

Body wears the smile of accomplishment,
The illusion of a Greek necessity

Flows in the scrolls of her toga,
Her bare

Feet seem to be saying:
We have come so far, it is over.

Each dead child coiled, a white serpent,
One at each little

Pitcher of milk, now empty.
She has folded

Them back into her body as petals
Of a rose close when the garden

Stiffens and odours bleed
From the sweet, deep throats of the night flower.

The moon has nothing to be sad about,
Staring from her hood of bone.

She is used to this sort of thing.
Her blacks crackle and drag.

The vision of death as composure, a work done well, is beautifully realized in the first four stanzas. The next several, with "Each dead child coiled,
a white serpent," seem to me to drop into a kind of sensationalism—not the
kind one finds in the confessional poems, with their alternating archness and
violence, but one that invokes the completion that may come once death is
done and finished. The penultimate stanza is very fine; the last lines again
seem forced.

Even in this kind of poetry, which does strike an original note, there are
many limitations. The poems often shock; they seldom surprise. They are
deficient in plasticity of feeling, the modulation of voice that a poet writing
out of a controlled maturity of consciousness can muster. Even the best of
Sylvia Plath's poems, as her admirer Stephen Spender admits, "have little
principle of beginning or ending, but seem fragments, not so much of one
long poem, as of an outpouring which could not stop with the lapsing of the
poet's hysteria."

Perhaps the hardest critical question remains. Given the fact that in a
few poems Sylvia Plath illustrates an extreme state of existence, one at the
very boundary of nonexistence, what illumination—moral, psychological,

social—can be provided of either this state or the general human condition by a writer so deeply rooted in the extremity of her plight? Suicide is an eternal possibility of our life and therefore always interesting; but what is the relation between a sensibility so deeply captive to the idea of suicide and the claims and possibilities of human existence in general? That her story is intensely moving, that her talent was notable, that her final breakthrough rouses admiration—of course! Yet in none of the essays devoted to praising Sylvia Plath have I found a coherent statement as to the nature, let alone the value, of her vision. Perhaps it is assumed that to enter the state of mind in which she found herself at the end of her life is its own ground for high valuation; but what will her admirers say to those who reply that precisely this assumption is what needs to be questioned?

After the noise abates and judgment returns, Sylvia Plath will be regarded as an interesting minor poet whose personal story was poignant. A few of her poems will find a place in anthologies—and when you consider the common fate of talent, that, after all, will not be a small acknowledgment.

D. F. McKAY

Aspects of Energy in the Poetry
of Dylan Thomas and Sylvia Plath

Great literature is simply language charged
with meaning to the utmost possible degree.
—EZRA POUND

Pound's concise description reflects not only upon the achievements of the
past but upon experiments undertaken in the present century. Like some
statements in *Hamlet*, Pound's is susceptible of various interpretations depending upon where one directs the falling stress. Perhaps it is true to
say that most modern experimental poets have been preoccupied with the
charge of language, the energy with which meaning is conveyed. In extreme
instances, to extend the generalization, energy consumes meaning the way
fire feeds on matter; projectivist poets, for example, might revise Pound's
statement to read "charged to the utmost possible degree," since it is within
poetic action itself that meaning is felt to reside.

The aesthetic problem sleeping in Pound's statement can give access to
the poetry of Sylvia Plath and Dylan Thomas, each of whom has been, on
occasion, judged deficient in terms of meaning. In Thomas's case the charge
is most frequently functional, involving his alleged failure to deliver (gratuitous obscurity, linguistic fraudulence), while Plath's content is often viewed
as pathologically disordered, though clear. Thomas's poetry, too, has been
interpreted by David Holbrook as the emanation of a schizoid individual. On
the other hand, neither poet, however meaningless or deranged, lacks vitality.
Since their poems are highly charged, they are difficult to forget, outgrow,
or dispense with critically. The fact that Mr. Holbrook in *Dylan Thomas:*

From *The Critical Quarterly* 16, no. 1 (Spring 1974). © 1974 by C. B. Cox.

The Code of Night (which contains numerous comparative references to Sylvia Plath) has come back to the poet exorcised in *Llareggub Revisited* testifies to the tenacity of the poetry even among inhospitable minds. Poetry which concentrates upon energy—its generation, control and unleashing— generally leaves readers with an exhilarating sense of kinesis, as skiing or flying does, but without a firm conception of content. It lives most fully in the act of reading, and recedes during the process of critical reflection when more tangible problems of "meaning" come naturally to the fore. Criticism of Thomas and Plath, dutifully focusing attention on the problem area of meaning, tends to relegate its energy—what it does—to the role of a stylistic enhancement to the poetry's literal signification. But such assumptions do not seem adequate to the art of either poet. Instead of construing the energy of the poem as the vehicle or corroborator of meaning, it may be more appropriate to keep another metaphor uppermost in mind: meaning as a conductor of energy, serving to deliver it as a wire conducts electricity. In terms of Pound's statement, we let the stress fall more heavily upon the word "charged."

An approach to poetic energy may take as starting point Ernest Fenollosa's seminal essay on the Chinese written character as a medium for poetry [printed in Ezra Pound's *Instigations*]. Arguing the felicity of the ideogram, Fenollosa points out that the relations between things, preserved intact by the Chinese character, are more real than the things they relate.

> Things are only the terminal points, or rather the meeting points of actions, cross-sections cut through actions, snap shots. Neither can a pure verb, an abstract motion, be possible in nature. The eye sees noun and verb as one: things in motion, motion in things, and so the Chinese conception tends to represent them.

In Western syntax, this simultaneity of agent-action-object is sacrificed; we dissociate the dancer from the dance and signify their relationship through word order. The language a poet uses creates order by abstracting from the reality he apprehends. In one sense, then, he must come to terms with an inherited prescriptive syntax. Both Thomas and Plath demonstrate a desire to regain the simultaneity of experience by the strategic manipulation of language: to bring together dancer, the act of dancing and the dance. It is a desire which, related to us on a thematic level, is acted out dramatically by the action of their poems.

Plath's "Ariel" is, on a superficial level, a poem about the experience of horseback riding at dawn.

Stasis in darkness.
Then the substanceless blue
Pour of tor and distances.

God's lioness,
How one we grow,
Pivot of heels and knees!

Ariel, the horse's name, is also the name given to the city of Jerusalem by Isaiah (Isa. 29:7) and means "God's lion." Here, deity is an immanent and coercive animal power, remorselessly pulling the rider out of her sense of personal identity and into a unity with itself. From the condition of stasis, produced, perhaps, by riding in the pre-dawn darkness where the sensation of speed is reduced because there is no visual gauge, the rider/poet leaps into a condition of absolute kinesis, as though a clutch had suddenly been released. The line "Stasis in darkness" aurally enacts the repetitive churn of the hooves, and "Pour of tor" blurs sounds just as the scenery is swept in "substanceless blue." The action peels objects from their substance while it weds the rider to her horse: the furrow which "splits and passes" is "sister to / The brown arc / Of the neck I cannot catch."

Reduced to its psychological content, the poem expresses a conventional death wish, a desire for extinction. But such a characterization of the poem ignores the exhilaration due not so much to the sensation of speed as to the new, purer reality which is momentarily achieved. The rider/poet becomes agent, act and object, a unity conveyed thematically, enacted verbally.

White
Godiva, I unpeel—
Dead hands, dead stringencies.

And now I
Foam to wheat, a glitter of seas.
The child's cry

Melts in the wall.
And I
Am the arrow,

The dew that flies
Suicidal, at one with the drive
Into the red

Eye, the cauldron of morning.

The linear thrust of the passage is enhanced by the obsessive "I" sounds, which connect the personal pronoun (I, White/Godiva of the rider) to both action (flies, drive), and its ultimate, obliterating, end (suicidal, red/Eye). Person, act and end are swept into the one driving force by the poet's aural strategy. At the same time, the line lengths are calculated to reinforce the dissolution of the unpeeling "I," which is twice left to dangle weakly at the end of the line, to be overwhelmed by the aggressive verbs which follow. The full stress falling upon "Am" in "Am the arrow" contributes to the sense of ontological awareness dawning, a new pulse in the insipid copula. The shift from "I" to the "Eye" of the rising sun appears to be a metaphysical yoking of disparates, but it is worked out in the passage by syntactical action; the emphasis shifts from the subject "I" through the action to the object "Eye," carrying the reader to this conclusion rather than forcing him into an intellectual leap.

Like most visionary experiences in which the protagonist is invaded by divine power, the flight into the sun constitutes the consummation of being as well as a destruction. Thomas's line "The sundering ultimate king-dom of genesis' thunder" at the conclusion of "Ceremony after a Fire Raid" delineates the contradictory constituents of such moments of pure energy. In "Ariel" we do not pause to distinguish "destructive" from "creative" aspects of the "cauldron of morning": it is a poem about energy itself. But while the energy in "Ariel" is divine, it is divinity incarnate, springing from physical event. To the simultaneity of agent, act and object, then, can be added the conjunction of divine and natural worlds, which the title "Ariel," God's lion, exemplifies. Like Yeats's "Leda and the Swan," "Ariel" deals with invasion by a power that is both spiritual and brute, but rendered as devastating per-sonal experience rather than myth. Nor does Plath stand back, as Yeats does, to introduce the question of consequences there engendered, although the headlong intensity of the poem leads one to suspect that they would be dire and glorious as those resulting from the violation of Leda, were the poet to add reflection to action.

Placed beside "Ariel," Thomas's "The force that through the green fuse drives the flower" seems at first an abstract declaration of the principles actively at work in Plath's poem. A single force which is creative and destruc-tive at the same time unifies the poet with the natural environment. But Thomas's poem, possessing a high degree of formal coherence, remains ca-denced and calm; it registers the unity conferred by the force more deeply than its vigour. Furthermore, there is little indication that the poet establishes identity with the force itself, as Plath does. He remains an essentially passive and "dumb" recipient.

> The force that through the green fuse drives the flower
> Drives my green age; that blasts the roots of trees
> Is my destroyer.
> And I am dumb to tell the crooked rose
> My youth is bent by the same wintry fever.

This is a different form of primitive energy from that experienced in "Ariel," expressing itself in the cyclic patterns of nature, with their balanced, inevitable rhythm. Thomas's syntax is not only balanced, countering each example of the force in nature with an example in the poet, but it repeats, stanza by stanza, the same sentence structure. (The alteration in the fourth stanza which begins "The lips of time leech to the fountain head," is possible because the balanced structure has been established by three iterations, and the equal application of the general statement to nature and to man can be assumed.) It exemplifies, then, something of nature's profound but regulated power; in Thomas's later poetry the sun is "ruled" and the sea "ramshackling." The use of half rhyme (flower-destroyer-fever) does provide an edge like a minor key within the formal regularities of the rhyme-scheme, but there is none of the nakedly dangerous power unleashed in "Ariel."

Thomas's metaphors exemplify the reassuring regularity of destructive and creative force: pulsation, systole and diastole, inhalation and exhalation. But in Plath's poetry, power can surge as suddenly as an opened artery; it suggests a breach of the natural order. "The blood jet," she declares in one of her last poems, "is poetry, / There is no stopping it." The lethal jungle cats which circulate through the imagery of *Ariel* and *Winter Trees* typify the feline movements of her metaphors, with their sudden pounces upon fresh revelations and their muscles rippling beneath the skin. Thomas more consistently invokes the basso continuo rhythms of existence relying, ponderously at times, upon the resonance of rhetoric. Time, his nemesis, "tracks you down," dogged and relentless; the mortal woe is chronic rather than acute.

Thomas's syntax does not always evince the expected regularity nor the coherence of "The force that through the green fuse drives the flower." In some instances, Donald Davie declares [in his book *Articulate Energy*], he exploits a "pseudo-syntax." "Formally correct, his syntax cannot mime, as it offers to do, a movement of the mind." Within the context of his argument, which he illustrates with the seventh "Altarwise by owl-light" sonnet, this is a telling criticism. But by considering the whole vision of the poet, it is possible to grasp the larger intelligibility of his syntactical manoeuvres. Syntax represents order and succession in the sentence, the spatio-temporal design.

Since Thomas, in the early poems (basically those published before 1940), generally takes the position of a humanity wronged, "double-crossed" by the natural order, it might be argued that an attack upon syntax constitutes the appropriate linguistic gesture. He does not, it should be noted, utterly discard syntax as extreme vers-librists have done, but manipulates an inexorable movement to his own ends. If the most pervasive trend in his poetry is to make "a merry manshape of your walking circle," to humanize an alien cosmos, then this verbal strategy is consistent, enacting the poet's equivocal relationship to the analogue in reality. In the later poetry, where Thomas has managed to "Suffer the heaven's children through my heartbeat," giving time and space a human shape, the problem of pseudo-syntax has, appropriately, evaporated. In "Fern Hill," time is the gentle warder, in whose chains the child is permitted to sing; in "Poem on his birthday" he exultantly sails out to die with the sun blooming and the world spinning "its morning of praise."

Thomas may have discovered in the aural euphony of these late poems a kind of supra-syntax, reconciling the subjective flow of images with the inflexible facts of order and succession embodied by normal syntax. In terms of Thomas's vision, the later poetry expresses beatific harmony between man and the stern conditions governing his existence. Certainly their flow of sound and meaning is in sharp contrast to his earlier work, which generates energies that, as Thomas noted, often exceed the limits of single poems and lead in the direction of a corporate meaning. One must ask whether any of Thomas's poems do offer to mime "a movement of the mind." Radically romantic in attitude, he is, like Rimbaud, devoted to the mind as renovator rather than recorder of mental reality. Since syntax represents in language the mundane order, it is here that poetic alterations must be made, and new movements undertaken.

Thomas, as has been implied, is concerned to develop a mythology of mankind. This is like the myth of Prometheus in the sense that he is striving to acquire fresh powers for man, but the Promethean defiance expressed in such poems as "I see the boys of summer" ("But seasons must be challenged or they totter / Into a chiming quarter") grows into the reconciliation noted in the later poems, a reconciliation reaching the intensity of epiphany in such poems as "Vision and Prayer." The energy of his poems is intrinsically more complex, too, than the simple gift of light and heat. Like fire in the myth of Meleager, it consumes the self that expresses it: "The force that through the green fuse drives the flower . . . is my destroyer." Thomas's allusion to Meleager in the second "Altarwise by owl-light" sonnet affirms this paradoxical identity of creative and destructive powers within the context of the individual life:

> Child of the short spark in a shapeless country
> Soon sets alight a long stick from the cradle.

The same poem, significantly, refers to the mother as "the planet-ducted pelican of circles" who "weans on an artery the gender's strip." Like Meleager's burning brand, the legendary sacrifice of the pelican, suckling her offspring on her heart's blood, exemplifies the consumptive condition of creative thrust. In the sonnets, and indeed in Thomas's poetry as a whole, this relationship prevails: the child's rise entails the parents' decline as surely as one bicycle pedal requires a complement.

The climax of the sonnets is achieved in sonnet "VIII" ("This was the crucifixion on the mountain") wherein the child-hero seizes the symbol of potency, his father's phallus, which enables him to "Suffer the heaven's children through my heartbeat." This signal act on reaching majority, then, is the apotheosis of the child, the crucifixion and castration of the father.

> I by the tree of thieves, all glory's sawbones,
> Unsex the skeleton this mountain minute,
> And by this blowclock witness of the sun
> Suffer the heaven's children through my heartbeat.

Attention is drawn to the Meleagrian paradox of "sawbones" (physician, castrator) and to "blowclock," which is a British word for a dandelion head gone to seed, dispersed by the blowing of children, and of course an oppressive time symbol which is detonated. It is also, trusting for a moment the referential value of "this," the old man's phallus, a symbol of potency which effects a sexual dispersal of seed as well.

Several sources lurk behind this passage. The phrase "unsex the skeleton" is borrowed from James Thomson's *The City of Dreadful Night.*

> The phantoms have no reticence at all:
> The nudity of flesh will blush through tameless,
> The extreme nudity of bone grins shameless,
> The unsexed skeleton mocks shroud and pall.

And the situation reflects the death of Heracles, whose role as the zodiacal hero is one aspect of the father's *persona.* In mortal agony from the poisoned tunic corroding his flesh, Heracles begs his son Hyllus to kill him. The boy sacrifices his father upon a funeral pyre—acting as destroyer and physician ". . . healer of my sufferings, sole physician of my pain" (Sophocles, *The Trachiniae,* trans. Richard C. Jebb).

Taking this as the main thematic line of the sequence, it is especially instructive to look again at the "pseudo-syntax" in which one would expect to find an analogous dynamic of energies. If the syntax of the sestet of the first sonnet is unravelled it reveals, not merely a series of richly ambiguous images clinging to the narrative thread, but two simultaneous and contrary narratives occupying the same syntactical structure. In substance, the father creates the child, the child destroys the father.

> Altarwise by owl-light in the half-way house
> The gentleman lay graveward with his furies;
> Abaddon in the hangnail cracked from Adam,
> And, from his fork, a dog among the fairies,
> The atlas-eater with a jaw for news,
> Bit out the mandrake with to-morrow's scream.

The ambiguity here pivots on the identity of "his" in line four. One reading makes "his fork" the loins of the father, and the phallus an uncouth, traditionally lustful, dog in the genteel fairy atmosphere of the womb. He bites out the mandrake, which, as a *homunculus* is the unborn child's body. The scream will occur to-morrow, with the pangs of birth. The "atlas-eater" recalls the father's cosmic role as the "long world's gentleman" at the end of this sonnet, a *roué* who shares his bed with the two females of the tropics, Capricorn and Cancer. A second reading makes "his fork" the child's springing up. The mandrake, then, is the father's phallus (following the usage in Donne's "Song") which the child bites out, foreshadowing tomorrow's apotheosis of sonnet "VIII" described above. In the next lines the father, already "penny-eyed" and a "gentleman of wounds" is characterized in the apposite synecdoche "old cock from nowheres." Consequently the child, being created by the father, is simultaneously the destroyer, the "atlas-eater" of this long world's gentleman. Taking these two narratives into account, the figures of Abaddon, the destroying angel of Revelation, and Adam are seen to represent functions which are filled equally by the father and the son, and not the fixed symbolic identities of either.

Without question the syntax in this passage is burdened beyond its capacity. But one must question whether the intent is solely the "enormous oneness . . . simultaneity in space-time and identification" which Elizabeth Sewell [in *The Structure of Poetry*] remarks in Thomas and Rimbaud, even though such may be the effect of the usual reading. The dual meaning forces two syntactical currents, or transfers of energy from agent through action to object, against one another, a sort of functional chiasmus.

father   son

creates/
destroys

son   father

This is a way of acting out in syntax the Meleagrian paradox embodied in the poem's symbolic content. Of course, this exemplary feat is not long sustained, but it does act as a paradigm for Thomas's strategy with syntax. He moves away from the transfer of a single impulse in one direction (agent-action-object) toward the concept of multiple exchanges, a field of forces rather than a line of energy. We are frequently left hunting for a "subject" to which the energies of the poem can be tied, and made accountable.

Thomas registers dissatisfaction with ordinary language at various points in the early poems. The alphabet, drawing upon the expression from old primers, is "the Christ-cross-row of death" which the child must learn by heart. Verbalization falsifies mental reality.

> And from the first declension of the flesh
> I learnt man's tongue, to twist the shapes of thoughts
> Into the stony idiom of the brain.

To outwit the stony idiom in verse, Thomas developed the metaphorical technique of interpenetrating attributes. Sometimes, at its least successful, this works as a rather mechanically transferred epithet: "the man in the wind and the west moon," "enamelled eyes and the spectacled claws." In other instances the attributes cross with a paradoxical necessity of their own.

> This flesh you break, this blood you let
> Make desolation in the vein,
> Were oat and grape
> Born of the sensual root and sap;
> My wine you drink, my bread you snap.

Thomas expounded this poetic principle, cuttingly, when commenting on one of Pamela Hansford Johnson's poems in a letter to her.

> The man who said, for the first time, "*I see the rose*," said nothing, but the man who said for the first time "*The rose sees me*" uttered a very wonderful truth. . . . By the magic of words and images you must make it clear to him that the relationships are real. And only in "My blood is drawn from the veins of the roses," do you provide any proof. You gave the rose a human vein, and you gave your own vein the blood of the rose; now that *is* relationship. "I am his son" means little compared with "I am his flesh and blood."
>
> (from *Selected Letters,* ed. Constantine FitzGibbon)

The line cannot simply assert relationships; it must create them within itself by this verbal torque, which forces alien entities to mingle, implicating them in each other. An extreme extension of the principle is the flow of contrary meanings through the syntax of "Altarwise by owl-light" sonnet "I."

And its presence should also be observed in the passage which Professor Davie has chosen to illustrate his objections.

> Time is the tune my ladies lend their heartbreak,
> From bald pavilions and the house of bread
> Time tracks the sound of shape on man and cloud,
> On rose and icicle the ringing handprint.

Without unduly explicating the many associations which accrue, it is worthwhile to examine the arousing and twisting of the reader's syntactical expectations in the passage. Time's determination of the structure of reality, tracking the "sound of shape" is, for readers of Thomas, axiomatic. The last two lines are balanced, the structure of the last line mirroring its predecessor, with the agent and action resting tacit: Time tracks the sound of shape on man and cloud / On rose and icicle [time tracks] the ringing handprint. This mirroring forces equivalences upon the reader. "On man and cloud" matches "on rose and icicle," and "sound of shape" matches "ringing (sound) handprint (shape)." Here, however, the reader is drawn up short, for if the impression stamped by tyrannical time is a handprint, man is implicated as the agent of time as well as its victim, by thematic and syntactic logic. The surprise throws us back to a central paradox of the sonnet. The ladies sing to express heartbreak from all stations of existence. ("Bald pavilions" suggests cold palaces and "the house of bread" is the meaning of Bethlehem, indicating the two poles, perhaps, of Christ's life.) But the act of lamentation for time's cruelty is conducted in time's own medium, a musical version of the Meleagrian paradox. Time is the tune itself, the substance, and not merely the boundary of being. This sonnet precedes the climactic crucifixion sonnet, with its blowclock and humanization of time. It appears to stand in relation to it as the penultimate or "leading" note in a scale. The deliberate confounding of man with time, epitomized by these ladies "with the teats of music" who are sirens ("scaled sea-sawers") and lamenting mothers at once, prepares the ground for the climax to follow. It is significant that even here, at the weakest point of the sonnets, the principle of interpenetration is at work.

The techniques generating energy in Thomas's poetry can all be traced back to the primal force, sometimes abstractly construed as time, as it is resisted, accepted or converted by man. The power present in Sylvia Plath's late poetry brooks no such domestication at man's hand; it suggests the sudden violence of wilderness rather than the inexorable passage of seasons across a pastoral landscape. Plath's earlier poems, published in *The Colossus* (1960) and posthumously collected in *Crossing the Water* frequently approach this power from the outside, awed. She seems, at this phase, to be summoning the forces that are later to course so intensely through *Ariel* and *Winter Trees*. Her own dissatisfied estimate is preserved in her poem "Stillborn."

> These poems do not live: it's a sad diagnosis.
> They grew their toes and fingers well enough,
> Their little foreheads bulged with concentration.
> If they missed out on walking about like people
> It wasn't for any lack of mother-love.

It need not be our estimate, for these poems are finely wrought and indeed highly concentrated. But, as she diagnoses, they do not move; they are saddled with a competence that creates stillness and the chill perfection, which, like that of the Munich mannequins, is terrible and cannot have children. Primitive environments in pre-*Ariel* poems such as "Two Campers in Cloud Country," "Hardcastle Crags," "Sleep in the Mojave Desert," and "Wuthering Heights" possess an energy she strongly desires to tap. In "Black Rook in Rainy Weather," she declares:

> I only know that a rook
> Ordering its black feathers can so shine
> As to seize my senses, haul
> My eyelids up, and grant
> A brief respite from fear
> Of total neutrality.

It is a period of "The long wait for the angel" as she describes her condition in the same poem, "For that rare, random descent." In one sense, this longing exemplifies a desire to return to an heroic age, to inhabit the psychic equivalent of wilderness: "Unlucky the hero born / In this province of the stuck record."

But there is a countervailing force in Plath's poetry which resists the divine energy of "Ariel" and proposes alternatives to the apocalypse of the self. "Tulips" offers a good introduction to this alternative, the ideal static world of the hospital, the museum, the Munich storefront, the morgue. The stasis, in fact, is a form of artifice, a stylized anti-life, cloistered as a convent from the brute uncertainty of natural existence: "I am a nun now, I have never been so pure." The tulips are a vociferous affront to this serenity, as grotesquely out of place as a real bird would be in Yeats's artifice of eternity.

The poem moves carefully, with the caution of convalescence, preserving balance in tone and rhythm.

> The tulips are too excitable, it is winter here.
> Look how white everything is, how quiet, how snowed-in.
> I am learning peacefulness, lying by myself quietly
> As the light lies on these white walls, this bed, these hands.

The measured pace is achieved by the similar phrasing in lines one and three, two and four, by repetitive diction emphasizing the absolute monotone of sound and monochrome of colour, and by the technique of cataloguing to avoid pushing the reader to any metaphorical leaps. Another poem, "Fever 103°," also concentrates on the purity we experience, like a preview of heaven, in sickness and convalescence. We seem to shed carnality.

> I am too pure for you or anyone.
> Your body
> Hurts me as the world hurts God.

It is common enough to observe that this denies life. Yet we must recognize that Plath is experiencing life undiluted, at an intensity that naturally provokes caution. It is a fearful thing to ride God's lion, the coercive force which, in "Tulips," she strives desperately to avoid.

> The tulips should be behind bars like dangerous animals;
> They are opening like the mouth of some great African cat.

Here God's lion is viewed from the outside, a dangerous predator seeking to drag you into mortality.

At different points in her poetry, each of these forms of energy lays claim to her allegiance. "Years" is another poem which places stasis and kinesis in opposition, and in a cosmological perspective. Basically, the poem presents a view of time and eternity. The years, like those of the orient, "enter as animals" from the outer space of a dark and frozen eternity. Here the poet declares sentiments in keeping with "Ariel," preferring "The piston in motion" and the "merciless churn" of the horses hooves to God's great emptiness.

> O God, I am not like you
> In your vacuous black,
> Stars stuck all over, bright stupid confetti.
> Eternity bores me,
> I never wanted it.

What, she demands, is so great in the "great stasis" of eternity? Yet the defiance is shrill, betraying the awesome lure of that frozen vacuity. And there is implicit recognition of the connection between the great Stasis and the kinesis of hoof and piston.

> Is it a tiger this year, this roar at the door?
> Is it a Christus,
> The awful
> God-bit in him
> Dying to fly and be done with it?

When eternity, abstract and boring, renders itself incarnate, the enormous energy of God's Lion, manifest in the tiger, the Christus, and Ariel surges forth. A stasis is, after all, a wheel spinning without resistance; the measure of its speed and power can only be taken when there is a landscape flying past, when it is labouring through the sludge of time and space. Hence the Christus, bearing a "God-bit" which may be intended to include an allusion to the bit in a horse's bridle, is "dying to fly and be done with it," to repeat Ariel's apocalypse in the sun.

The two forms of energy have consequences for spatial perception as well. The tulips in the hospital room insist upon themselves, an erupting focal point in the featureless surface of her attention. Visually they represent the arrival of dramatic, coercive perspective in a stylized, iconic realm. The insistence of the tulips is verbally acted out in the repetition of "snags and eddies," which snags the smooth flow of the otherwise flaccid diction, and in the sudden particularity of the startling rust-red engine.

> Now the air snags and eddies round them the way a river
> Snags and eddies round a sunken rust-red engine.
> They concentrate my attention, that was happy
> Playing and resting without committing itself.

Something similar occurs in "Morning Song," where the newly born child enters as a "New statue" in the draughty museum, focusing attention upon himself and threatening the safety of the older residents, who "stand round blankly as walls." The stasis of the deist universe is suggested by his conception: "Love set you going like a fat gold watch"; but, like the years, he develops animal traits when incarnate: "Your mouth opens clean as a cat's." The poem is singular for its finely sustained tone, neither sentimental nor desperate, yet full of the awe due such mysterious invaders. The arrival is "magnified" by the voices echoing in the museum, an expression which astutely collects the Magnificat of Mary into the poem's ambit. Another birth poem, "Nick and the Candlestick," similarly combines an allusion to the nativity with the conception of a new, authoritative visual perspective.

> You are the one
> Solid the spaces lean on, envious.
> You are the baby in the barn.

While this form of ordering prompts and directs action, its complementary opposite withdraws the stimulus and erases the perspective, letting the "envious spaces" take over. In "The Rival" the antagonist contrives to petrify reality.

> And your first gift is making stone out of everything.
> I wake to a mausoleum; you are here,
> Ticking your fingers on the marble table, looking for cigarettes,
> Spiteful as a woman, but not so nervous,
> And dying to say something unanswerable.

In Plath's poetry, the forces possess, and will not be possessed, or tamed, themselves. In "Daddy," the composite figure, reminiscent of Aleister Crowley, but with attributes drawn from the concentration camp commandant, Satan, and Dracula, must be exorcised with a "stake in your fat black heart." But one wakes to the startling realization that Daddy's victim has become, through the process of exorcism, as terrible as her tormentor—a Lady Lazarus who courts death and destroys husbands as the surrogates of her father. The ontological predicament, as with Thomas, recalls Meleager's burning brand, and due to the two forms of energy manifest in her poetry, is still more fraught with latent paradox. If one avoids, with stylized artifice, the devastation attendant upon Ariel's absolute drive, one is simply circumventing the act of dying by constructing a kind of death-in-life. But to yield to the driving piston and hoof is to affirm and feed the fires of mortality. To cancel the black beast's claim on the spirit, you must dabble in monstrosity yourself. Surely this constitutes a pathology of the human condition and not solely of the agonized self which so articulately registers its stress. Though Plath's bare content has the exotic appeal of the sensational private confession, the active ingredients bespeak psychic discoveries to which the reader reacts first with a shock of recognition, before he settles, more comfortably, into a posture of judgement.

Discussing the art of redemption in Plath's poetry, Andrew Brink draws attention to the absence of regenerative elements.

> Thus it is a downward curve we are describing, not a complete
> cycle with a new upswing after bottom has been touched. The

urge to begin again is certainly present but the poems show no source of outside energy to activate the archetypes—no love and no forgiveness. With this essential ingredient missing the myth of eternal return, the engendering and making new, is all but invalidated.

The religious terminology of redemption and damnation sits uncomfortably in the context of Plath's sensibility. Perhaps the primitive tabu, indicating undifferentiated puissance (the French *sacré*—cursed and holy at once) more closely approximates her attitude to power; one of the epithets applied to "Daddy" is "a bag full of God." It is also questionable whether the archetypes in her poetry are being exploited for their standard psychological and mythological value. Certainly they do not behave with the antique dependability of Vernon Watkins's or Kathleen Raine's water-smoothed stones. One senses, rather, that the stock symbols—the black boot, yew tree, moon, magi, changeling, muse, Persephone—are presented, in the company of vivid original metaphors, for dissection. (Words, in the poem of that title, are "axes," a metaphor which ingeniously combines their cutting edge and concussive value with the idea of planes of meaning.) For if man can become conscious of his archetypes, and Plath most assuredly is, he can also become bored with them, and impatient with their tendency to conceal while ostensibly revealing, like the Delphic oracle. In "The Hanging Man," a poem about divine visitation which suggests shock therapy, she dwells upon the aftermath—the curse of complete awareness.

> By the roots of my hair some god got hold of me.
> I sizzled in his blue volts like a desert prophet.
> The nights snapped out of sight like a lizard's eyelid:
> A world of bald white days in a shadeless socket.
> A vulturous boredom pinned me in this tree.
> If he were I, he would do what I did.

Having tasted this tabu, the blue volts of divine energy, she cannot then return to mundane life unchanged. In fact, reality is blighted by this cruel floodlight of awareness, and the succouring darkness is "snapped out of sight." It is the consequence, the "vulturous boredom," that seems to accompany many of her symbols, as though energy were to scorn its own productions, already leaving them in its wake like ballast. As the impotent visionary, the hanging man, Plath frequently delivers poems with a sardonic facility that is at once arrogant and anguished. Although there are, as Mr. Brink affirms, no redemptive elements in her poetry, there is a form of relief in renewed contact with the source of energy. In "Poppies in October," for in-

stance, the poppies are "a love gift" which, "unasked for" itself, provokes
the ultimate ontological question that fills and empties being at once.

> O my God, what am I
> That these late mouths should cry open
> In a forest of frost, in a dawn of cornflowers.

Invocation, resistance, allegiance, submission, exorcism: there is a spectrum of response to energy within which many modulations are possible. In general, it may be observed that Plath's poetic experience takes in the extremes, invoking the absent afflatus and transmitting the potency of a dominating animus, while Thomas variously resists and allies himself with a primal force. Considering the powers native to their poems is like becoming familiar with the climate of different countries; it will not answer questions of meaning in detail, but it helps to explain why such fauna and flora thrive within their frontiers.

STAN SMITH

Attitudes Counterfeiting Life:
The Irony of Artifice
in Sylvia Plath's The Bell Jar

The material of Sylvia Plath's only novel, *The Bell Jar* (1963), is conspicuously autobiographical, as recent anecdotal memoirs have revealed. But the book is more than a case-history of the attempted suicide and psychiatric treatment of a sensitive girl with literary ambition. It is a highly and originally structured novel, which has transmuted its raw material in a manner consonant with Plath's own comments on the relationship between art and personal experience:

> I believe one should be able to control and manipulate experience, even the most terrifying—like madness, being tortured, this kind of experience—and one should be able to manipulate these experiences with an informed and intelligent mind. I think that personal experience shouldn't be a kind of shut box and mirror-looking narcissistic experience. I believe it should be generally relevant.

The main principle of control in *The Bell Jar,* I wish to argue, lies precisely in the manipulation of a series of contrasts and analogies between "personal experience" and a variety of forms of "artifice."

One of the ways in which an experience can be made "generally relevant" has been suggested by Brecht, in his description of the "estrangement effect," ("*Verfremdungseffekt*"), which he contrasts with "empathy" ("*Einfühlung*"). "Empathy" invites the audience to collapse the distance between itself and the events depicted, to participate self-indulgently in a "mirror-looking narcissistic experience." The "estrangement effect," on the

From *The Critical Quarterly* 17, no. 3 (Autumn 1975). © 1975 by C. B. Cox.

other hand, establishes a distance between audience and event, in order to demonstrate that this action is not a metaphysical absolute, in which all participate as private sufferers, but an historically situated condition, towards which one can take a critical stance. To see the naturalistically depicted present, not as an absolute, but as an evanescent moment of history, is to invest it with the relativity with which the anthropologist endows an alien culture:

> Whoever has looked with astonishment at the eating customs, the jurisprudence, the love life of savage peoples, will also be able to look at our eating customs, our jurisprudence and our love life with astonishment.
>
> (trans. Darko Suvin)

In *The Bell Jar,* Sylvia Plath uses the psychological alienation of the heroine, Esther Greenwood, to reinforce this *aesthetic* alienation. Esther's "madness" offers her an increasingly "objective," exterior view of the "eating customs, jurisprudence, and love life" of the culture she has inherited. "Manners" provide an important motif of the book. Using the finger-bowl at a special lunch, Esther, for example, "thought what a long way [she] had come," and recalls that in her first encounter with a finger bowl, she drank the water and the cherry blossoms in it because "I thought it must be some clear sort of Japanese after-dinner soup." Esther's "oddity" is here revealed as, in origin, no more than a social disjunction, between her own learnt expectations and the codes of manners within which she comes increasingly to move. A clue to the process at work is revealed in her memory of a poet who in "do[ing] something incorrect at table with a certain arrogance," "made eating salad with your fingers seem to be the only natural and sensible thing to do." The poet, significantly, had been talking about "the antithesis of nature and art." Esther's perception of the fictive nature of "manners" spills over into an attitude which evacuated the world of all spontaneous content. There are no such things as "natural" responses, no intrinsic values in things, all are equally arbitrary and artificial, and all are viewed with the same cynical-naïve eye. Collapsing the "antithesis of nature and art," Esther comes to view her own life as an aesthetic construct, a perpetual self-manipulation, learning, like the babies she sees at the clinic, "all the little tricky things it takes to grow up, step by step, into an anxious and unsettling world."

The prospect of losing her virginity, for example, is viewed with the same voyeuristic frisson she brings to lesser events:

> The more I thought about it the better I liked the idea of being seduced by a simultaneous interpreter in New York City. . . .

And there would be a pleasant irony in sleeping with a man
Mrs. Willard had introduced me to, as if she were, in a round-
about way, to blame for it.

When this actually happens she feels "part of a great tradition," and it is
with a man she chooses to see as "a kind of impersonal, priest-like official,
as in the tales of tribal rites." Such a proclivity had always been a part of
Esther's identity—

> I had a way of persuading my Class Dean to let me do irregular
> things. She regarded me as a sort of interesting experiment.

> I began to feel pleased at my cleverness. I thought I only need tell
> him what I wanted to, and that I could control the picture he had
> of me by hiding this and revealing that, all the while he thought
> he was so smart,

and extends into her "cured" state—

> I decided to practise my new, normal personality on this man
> who, in the course of my hesitations, told me his name was Irwin.
> . . . It was only after seeing Irwin's study that I decided to seduce
> him.

Esther's paranoia penetrates the bland benevolent surfaces of other people's
motives to discover their inner and unconscious significance. The first psy-
chiatrist she visits, for example, is far less perceptive about her than she is
about him:

> His eyelashes were so long and thick they looked artificial. Black
> plastic reeds fringing two green, glacial pools.
>   Doctor Gordon's features were so perfect he was almost pretty.
> . . . He was young and good-looking, and I could see right away
> he was conceited.
>   Doctor Gordon had a photograph on his desk, in a silver frame,
> that half faced my leather chair. It was a family photograph, and
> it showed a beautiful dark haired woman, who could have been
> Doctor Gordon's sister, smiling out over the heads of two blond
> children. . . .
>   For some reason the photograph made me furious. I didn't see
> why it should be turned half towards me unless Doctor Gordon
> was trying to show me right away that he was married to some
> glamorous woman and I'd better not get any funny ideas.

What Esther observes here—and it is a recurring note throughout the book—
is the artificiality, the *artifice,* of Dr. Gordon's identity. He is an image
presented to the world, acting a conventional role. The photograph is a mirror (throughout the book the two images interweave) in which Dr. Gordon
admires his own reflection, for even his wife is a self-projection, a kind of
narcissistic twin.

Esther's stance towards her own self is graphically depicted in a sequence in the Public Gardens where, watching children riding a swanboat,
she recalls her own manipulated childhood:

> Everything I looked at seemed bright and extremely tiny.
>
> I saw, as if through the keyhole of a door I couldn't open,
> myself and my younger brother, knee high and holding rabbit-
> eared balloons, climb aboard a swanboat and fight for a seat at
> the edge, over the peanut-shell-paved water. My mouth tasted of
> cleanness and peppermint. If we were good at the dentist's my
> mother always bought us a swanboat ride.

She continually assumes the role of an aesthetic voyeur towards her own past
and present experience:

> I wanted to see as much as I could.
>
> I liked looking on at other people in crucial situations. If there
> was a road accident or a street fight or a baby pickled in a labo-
> ratory jar for me to look at, I'd stop and look so hard I never
> forgot it.
>
> I certainly learned a lot of things I never would have learned
> otherwise this way, and even when they surprised me or made
> me sick I never let on, but pretended that's the way I knew things
> were all the time.

The straightforward, callous prose is here undercut by currents of powerful
irony which subvert the whole disinterested stance. For the aestheticism is
redefined, implicitly, as the rationalized fear and insecurity of a pathological squeamishness, a social strategy that insulates one from feelings which
expose and entrap. Omniscience is redefined as a pose assumed to evade the
suspicion of callowness and ignorance.

This fastidious aesthetic distance extends, too, to the apparently "cured"
and regenerate Esther who is the imputed author of *The Bell Jar.* The book
itself supposedly fulfils that ambition to write a novel whose frustration con-
tributed to the breakdown it records. If the younger Esther stands in schizoid
relation to her own experiences, retrospectively analysing and interpreting
them, endlessly turning them over in her mind in some kind of Proustian

recherche, Esther the narrator assumes the same kind of stance to her past, seen as an initiation rite to be scrupulously and objectively tabulated. Plath, the actual author, seems to be manipulating a continuous and ironic parallel between the condition of schizophrenic self-alienation and the familiar devices of narrative technique. Esther's narrative distance from the recounted facts of her own previous life has a peculiar, antiseptic quality, presenting the most harrowing and intimate experiences with a dispassionateness which tends to endorse her own doubts about the extent of her cure. The hardboiled narrative tone suggests a narrator herself numbed in some significant way, left cold by her own past. If the younger Esther once felt as if she were "sitting under the same glass bell jar, stewing in my own sour air," while the world "flashed by like an improbable postcard," Esther the narrator seems preoccupied with insulating her own past self under the bell jar of a retrospective fiction. Plath not only enables us to see the pathological honesty of vision which accompanies and in part causes the younger Esther's breakdown; she also suggests that the assurance embodied in the posture of the disinterested narrator may itself have more profound social significance, and closer analogies with the schizophrenic's experience, and with the self-alienation of a world that dismisses that experience as mere delusion, than we appreciate. This double "estrangement effect" acts as a critical, ironic dimension in the novel.

One way in which the character Esther tries to reject the role to which she has been assigned and assume a manipulative power over others, is to invent a surrogate identity. It is clear that, initially, she sees it as a kind of authorial intervention in the plot of her own life, that gives her the opportunity to dissociate herself from the actions she commits, as the novelist employs a *persona* to establish a critical distance between himself and his narrative. Assuming the *persona* of an imaginary Chicago orphan, "Elly Higginbottom," whose faintly ludicrous name becomes a private joke at the expense of her victims, Esther feels a godlike invulnerability. "Elly" is invented on the spur of the moment, at the beginning of the novel, when Esther and her friend Doreen are picked up by Lenny, a disc-jockey, and his innocuous companion. Esther immediately feels marginal and insecure in this company, "gawky and morbid as somebody in a side-show." While Doreen has, quite literally, taken the limelight, Esther compensates by turning her sideshow into a private theatre, with a first night for her new *dramatis persona:*

> It was so dark in the bar I could hardly make out anything except
> Doreen. With her white hair and white dress she was so white
> she looked silver. I think she must have reflected the neons over

the bar. I felt myself melting into the shadows like the negative of
a person I'd never seen before in my life. . . .

"My name's Elly Higginbottom," I said. "I come from Chicago."
After that I felt safer. I didn't want anything I said or did that
night to be associated with me and my real name and coming
from Boston.

Her actual identity becomes no more than the negative source of her
positive image (Elly). Equipped with this *persona,* she assumes the heightened acuity of Stephen Dedalus's artist, "like the God of creation, invisible,
refined out of existence, indifferent, paring his finger-nails," in *The Portrait
of the Artist as a Young Man.* The vodka, she says, "made me feel powerful
and godlike"; by continuing to ignore her partner she dismisses him from
the script:

"I better go now," Frankie said, standing up. I couldn't see him
very clearly, the place was so dim, but for the first time I heard
what a high, silly voice he had. Nobody paid him any notice.

The Joycean connection is ratified on the later occasion when Esther revives
"Elly Higginbottom," in her encounter with a young sailor on Boston Common. For the sailor, she furnishes Elly with a fictitious past; for herself, Elly
is endowed with a speculative future which cancels out the predetermined
plot:

I thought if I ever did get to Chicago, I might change my name to
Elly Higginbottom for good. . . .
    In Chicago people would take me for what I was. I would be
simple Elly Higginbottom, the orphan. People would love me for
my sweet, quiet nature. They wouldn't be after me to read books
and write long papers on the twins in James Joyce.

Esther had at one point contemplated a thesis on "images about twins" in
Finnegans Wake. "Elly" is herself a kind of imaginary Joycean twin, behind
whom Esther can shelter, in order to observe with aesthetic disinterestedness
the behaviour of "her" characters. That this subterfuge does not work soon
becomes clear. While Lenny and Doreen jitterbug—

I sat cross-legged on one of the beds and tried to look devout and
impassive like some businessmen I once saw watching an Algerian
belly-dancer, but as soon as I leaned back against the wall under
the stuffed rabbit, the bed started to roll into the room, so I sat

down on a bearskin on the floor and leaned back against the bed
instead.

The simile establishes the discrepancy between the assumed indifference and
the prurience it scarcely conceals; it also shows Esther characteristically
watching the audience rather than the act, thus reinforcing the morbid self-
consciousness beneath the unruffled exterior. The uncooperative bed merely
confirms the failure of the pose, so that, very rapidly—

> I felt myself shrinking to a small black dot. . . . I felt like a hole
> in the ground.

This spurious authorial detachment is, in her own words, "de-
moralizing":

> It's like watching Paris from an express caboose heading in
> the opposite direction—every second the city gets smaller and
> smaller, only you feel it's really you getting smaller and smaller
> and lonelier and lonelier, rushing away from all those lights and
> that excitement at about a million miles an hour.

Against this depressing reality—of exclusion, marginality—the impassive
narrative voice of Esther—both as character and "author"—has to reassert
itself:

> I noticed, in the routine way you notice the colour of somebody's
> eyes, that Doreen's breasts had popped out of her dress and were
> swinging out like full brown melons as she circled belly-down
> on Lenny's shoulder, thrashing her legs in the air and screeching,
> and then they both started to laugh and slow up, and Lenny was
> trying to bite Doreen's hip through her skirt when I let myself
> out of the door before anything more could happen and managed
> to get down the stairs by leaning with both hands on the banister
> and half sliding the whole way.

The paratactic style of the reportage in its deliberate "routine way" attempts
to contain the emotional reaction apparent in the panicky headlong flight
which the movement of the sentence enacts. Returning to the hotel, Esther
experiences once more the sense of reality as a two-dimensional fiction:

> the city hung in my window, flat as a poster, glittering and blink-
> ing, but it might just as well not have been there at all, for all the
> good it did me.

From this point onwards, her perception of the world as an unreal back-
cloth for an unreal identity recurs, as her alienation deepens. From the train
window returning home to Boston, for example, she sees her own ghostly
reflection almost "refined out of existence," superimposed on an external
landscape which itself seems merely a stopped film:

> A wan reflection of myself, white wings, brown ponytail and all,
> ghosted over the landscape.
>   "Pollyanna Cowgirl," I said out loud.
>   A woman in the seat opposite looked up from her magazine.
> . . . I didn't really see why people should look at me. Plenty of
> people looked queerer than I did. . . .
>   The domesticated wilderness of pine, maple and oak rolled to a
> halt and stuck in the frame of the train window like a bad picture.

Recurrently, the desire to be a disinterested narrator comes up against
the obstructive reality of a world of others who can reduce the rebellious
self to "a small black dot." Persuaded to attend a party by Doreen, Esther
insists on her uninvolvement: " 'I am an observer,' I told myself, as I watched
Doreen being handed into the room by the blond boy to another man." Yet
she is immediately naïvely fascinated by the diamond stickpin of Marco, the
man with whom she is paired—"I couldn't take my eyes off that stickpin."
Perception is not a disinterested act—"It dazzled and danced with light like
a heavenly ice-cube"; and when Marco gives it to her, she is at once com-
promised, the observed of all observers—"I looked round. The faces were
as empty as plates, and nobody seemed to be breathing." Marco's attentions
are dehumanizing and reductive, and the glass of the bell jar does not protect
her from his thinly veiled malevolence:

> Marco's small, flickering smile reminded me of a snake I'd teased
> in the Bronx Zoo. When I tapped my finger on the stout cage
> glass the snake had opened its clockwork jaws and seemed to
> smile. Then it struck and struck at the invisible pane till I moved
> off.

He assumes a proprietorial, authorial power over her, making her dance
with him in a way which turns her into a puppet, "without any will or
knowledge of my own," and finally beating her up and attempting to rape
her. Significantly, she comes to think of him as a kind of *deus ex machina*:

> I began to see why woman-haters could make such fools of
> women. Woman-haters were like gods, invulnerable and chock-

full of power. They descended, and then they disappeared. You could never catch one.

The sense of being a character in someone else's fiction intensifies with Esther's return home to Boston. The telephone becomes a navel-string of obligation, tying her in to a world she would rather renounce, and a puppet string that can be tugged to call her to attention and performance. To avoid identification she assumes, in replying to the phone, "a low, disguised voice"; but, deflatingly, the caller mistakes this "*persona*" for laryngitis. As she speaks, the assumed "hollow voice" takes on an imperious autonomy, until it dictates to its author, cancelling her actual desire to register for some other course at a summer school.

When she reaches to the phone to reverse this decision she comes up against the glass of the bell jar, as if some external narrator, who had just spoken through her, had also prescribed the limits of her freedom:

> My hand advanced a few inches, then retreated and fell limp. I forced it towards the receiver again, but again it stopped short, as if it had collided with a pane of glass.

The same ventriloquial voice can cancel all her other options, while she helplessly listens on:

> I dialled the Admissions Office and listened to the zombie voice leave a message that Miss Esther Greenwood was cancelling all arrangements to come to summer school.

In revolt, she decides to spend the summer writing a novel.

Yet her motives for writing the novel are impure, as her comment—"That would fix a lot of people"—suggests. In part, she is interested in revenge; she will elicit from them the respect they should have given her before by "fixing" them (perhaps there is a lurking photographic pun here) as characters in a scenario over which she will have complete mastery. For the novel is to be explicitly and directly autobiographical. Its protagonist, "Elaine," is another surrogate—"Elly Higginbottom," possibly, endowed with the dignity of her full Christian name. "Elaine" is explicitly a self-projection:

> A feeling of tenderness filled my heart. My heroine would be myself, only in disguise. She would be called Elaine. Elaine.

Esther, however, lacks the critical distance from her character that both the imputed and the actual author of *The Bell Jar* possess. She is altogether absorbed in her heroine, unable to do more than transcribe her own actual

experience at the moment of writing. And yet even to do this she is forced
to stand back from herself in a way which heightens her self-estrangement,
spying upon herself as if she were a prying neighbour such as Mrs Ockenden,
or her own mother. She cannot progress beyond the first paragraph, and no
doubt if she could she would set up an infinite regress of heroines writing
about heroines. Her psychological problem becomes focussed, thus, in the
technical, literary impasse:

> Back on the breezeway, I fed the first, virgin sheet into my old
> portable and rolled it up.
>
> From another, distanced mind, I saw myself sitting on the
> breezeway, surrounded by two white clapboard walls, a mock
> orange bush and a clump of birches and a box hedge, small as a
> doll in a doll's house. . . .
>
> I sat like that for about an hour, trying to think what would
> come next, and, in my mind, the barefoot doll in her mother's
> old yellow nightgown sat and stared into space as well.
>
> "Why, honey, don't you want to get dressed?"
>
> My mother took care never to tell me to do anything. She
> would only reason with me sweetly, like one intelligent, mature
> person with another.
>
> "It's almost three in the afternoon."
>
> "I'm writing a novel," I said. "I haven't got time to change out
> of this and change into that."
>
> I lay on the couch on the breezeway and shut my eyes. I could
> hear my mother clearing the typewriter and the papers from the
> card-table and laying out the silver for supper, but I didn't move.

The teasingly apposite insinuation of Thackeray's famous conclusion to
Vanity Fair, as her mother packs away typewriter and papers, works both
ways. For if "Elaine" stands in dependent relation to her author, Esther in
turn feels herself the puppet of powers she cannot comprehend, as if she
too were a character in a novel (Plath's further irony is that of course she
is). But the "narrator" of this "novel"—Esther's life—is a whole matrix of
social forces, of conventions and norms represented by her mother's authorial manipulations, which have converged to make Esther precisely the person she is.

The image of the doll in the doll's-house reinforces this impression. The
world of *The Bell Jar* is full of such images. Hilda, one of Esther's companions in New York, is a puppet whose strings are pulled by the regulating
norms of an image-conscious and conformist society:

The night before I'd seen a play where the heroine was possessed
by a dybbuk, and when the dybbuk spoke from her mouth its
voice sounded so cavernous and deep you couldn't tell whether it
was a man or a woman. Well Hilda's voice sounded just like the
voice of that dybbuk.

   She stared at her reflection in the glossed shop windows as if
to make sure, moment by moment, that she continued to exist.

Hilda is doubly unreal. She is compared, not just to a person possessed
by a dybbuk, but to a character in a play so possessed—a fictional being. Her
moral observations are likewise products of the ethos of "fashion blurbs,
silver and full of nothing," in which she lives. She is a "mannequin," mere
clothes over an emptiness, lived by her society as if it were a possessing
dybbuk, needing perpetual ratification from its mirrors.

   Esther's most intense perception of the extent to which individuals are
the manipulated dummies of a puppet-master society occurs on her visit to
Dr. Gordon's mental hospital. She is bothered that "everything about the
house seemed normal, although I knew it must be chock-full of crazy people."
The individual instances imply a generic pattern, for the living-room seems
"the replica of a lounge in a guest house I visited once." Indeed, the place is
a parody of normality, an ensemble of isolated vignettes which together act
as an ironic commentary upon the "normal" world. Most significant is the
sense of display:

   Then my gaze slid over the people to the blaze of green beyond
   the diaphanous curtains, and I felt as if I were sitting in the window of an enormous department store. The figures around me
   weren't people, but shop dummies, painted to resemble people
   and propped up in attitudes counterfeiting life.

It is only their apparent immobility that distinguishes these people, as if their
abnormality lies simply in the isolation and endless repetition of any one of
a number of "normal" actions. "Insanity" is merely a still copy of sanity,
isolating and exposing its strangeness. The "schizoid" character parodies the
process by which "normal" identity is learnt from the imitation of images,
assimilating not only the content but the form of the image, acquiring the
stillness of the photograph which is a leitmotif of the book. Madness aspires
to the condition of art, recalling Stephen Dedalus's definition of the aesthetic
stance in *Portrait of the Artist:* "The aesthetic emotion . . . is therefore static.
The mind is arrested and raised above desire and loathing."

   The leitmotifs of photograph and puppet converge when Esther is expected, as part of her *Ladies' Day* commitment, to be photographed "with

props to show what we wanted to be." Reluctantly, she offers "poet" as her self-definition, and is equipped with a rose for the part. The scene becomes theatrical, as she looks through "a frieze of rubber plants" in the window to the sky where "a few stagey cloud puffs were travelling from right to left":

> The photographer fiddled with his hot white lights. "Show us how happy it makes you to write a poem." . . . .
> I felt it was very important to keep the line of my mouth level.
> "Give us a smile."
> At last, obediently, like the mouth of a ventriloquist's dummy, my own mouth started to quirk up.
> "Hey," the photographer protested, with sudden foreboding, "you look like you're going to cry."
> I couldn't stop.

With the onset of genuine emotion, the whole flimsy artificial scene collapses, as if the photographer and the magazine's literary editor, "Jay Cee," were themselves tormenting dybbuks exorcised only by the sight of *real* tears:

> When I lifted my head, the photographer had vanished.
> Jay Cee had vanished as well. I felt limp and betrayed, like the skin shed by a terrible animal, but it seemed to have taken my spirit with it, and everything else it could lay its paws on.

The photograph propagates a cult of individualism while actually negating it. For it is not the actual Esther but the cliché image that can be made from her which matters. She has become no more than a cipher in the life-process of a mass-circulation magazine, plucked momentarily out of anonymity to be invested with the fraudulent charisma of "celebrity" whose image then returns to its place of origin divested and purified of circumstantial history. Significantly, in the mental asylum later, she refuses to admit that a picture in a magazine may be of her. The photograph, the magazine, popsong, film and novel all become vehicles for propagating a pattern of manners which are themselves fictive structurings of reality. The romantic novels of Philomena Guinea, whose scholarship Esther wins, are, for example,

> crammed from beginning to end with long, suspenseful questions: "Would Evelyn discern that Gladys knew Roger in her past? wondered Hector feverishly" and "How could Donald marry her when he learned of the child Elsie, hidden away with Mrs Rollmop on the secluded country farm? Griselda demanded of her bleak, moonlit pillow."

This debased art falls recurrently into pastiche of itself, becoming a self-parasitic genre which seeks its ratification by reference to an autonomous, counterfeit world of "conventional" images and "artificial" expectations.

A film Esther watches is no more than a copy of other films, its heroines imitations of other heroines, even its actresses imitations of actresses:

> The movie was very poor. It starred a nice blond girl who looked like June Allyson but was really somebody else, and a sexy black-haired girl who looked like Elizabeth Taylor but was also somebody else, and two big, broad-shouldered bone-heads with names like Rick and Gil.

Its "conventional" nature as "a football romance . . . in technicolour" makes the film absolutely predictable:

> Finally I could see the nice girl was going to end up with the nice football hero and the sexy girl was going to end up with nobody, because the man named Gil had only wanted a mistress and not a wife all along and was now packing off to Europe on a single ticket.

When she first contemplates suicide, Esther's "chorus of voices" indict her for having a similarly factitious image. Each reproach involves exposure and fixing:

> *Doesn't your work interest you, Esther?*
> *You know, Esther, you've got the perfect set-up of a true neurotic.*
> *You'll never get anywhere like that, you'll never get anywhere like that, you'll never get anywhere like that.*
> Once, on a hot summer night, I had spent an hour kissing a hairy, ape-shaped law student from Yale because I felt sorry for him, he was so ugly.
> When I had finished, he said, "I have you taped, baby. You'll be a prude at forty."
> "Factitious!" my creative writing professor at college scrawled on a story of mine called "The Big Weekend."
> I hadn't known what factitious meant, so I looked it up in the dictionary.
> Factitious, artificial, sham.
> *You'll never get anywhere like that.*

This "cul-de-sac" of artifice is that inertia shared by both Esther and
"Elaine": a dead end in which art cannot grow because life itself has become
fixated in a counterfeit attitude. Esther sees suicide not so much as self-
destruction as a theatrical ritual which will free her from her "factitious"
identity and restore her to singularity. It is her "image" that she wishes to
murder, the fraudulent twin which is her public *persona,* a shamming and
artificial "dybbuk":

> But when it came right down to it, the skin of my wrist looked
> so white and defenceless that I couldn't do it. It was as if what
> I wanted to kill wasn't in that skin or the thin blue pulse that
> jumped under my thumb, but somewhere else, deeper, more se-
> cret, and a whole lot harder to get at. . . .
>
> I moved in front of the medicine cabinet. If I looked in the
> mirror while I did it, it would be like watching somebody else, in
> a book or a play.
>
> But the person in the mirror was paralysed and too stupid to
> do a thing

If the mirror-image here, like "Elly Higginbottom" and "Elaine," is a fictitious twin, the book also has its quota of real-life "twins." Joan Gilling,
an old rival for Esther's boyfriend, is admitted to the same mental hospital
where Esther is recovering from a later, almost successful suicide attempt.
As Esther had attempted to imitate a starlet's suicide described in the news-
papers so Joan in turn had imitated her, and she produces "a pile of clip-
pings" of the news-items which stirred her to admiration and imitation.

At times, Joan, in her bizarre mimicry of Esther, seems an externalized
fantasy. Her room, Esther notes, "was a mirror image of my own," and when
Joan at first recovers more rapidly than Esther, she becomes an objective
correlative of Esther's own self-criticism, a more successful twin with whom
Esther finds herself in sibling-rivalry:

> Joan had walk privileges, Joan had shopping privileges, Joan had
> town privileges. I gathered all my news of Joan into a little, bitter
> heap, though I received it with surface gladness. Joan was the
> beaming double of my old best self, specially designed to follow
> and torment me.

But Esther learns to distinguish the mythic image from the more complex
reality; to distinguish between copy and imitation, sameness and similarity;
and to see that there is a crucial failure of discrimination in confusing another
person with one's own projected image:

Her thoughts were not my thoughts, nor her feelings my feelings, but we were close enough so that her thoughts and feelings
seemed a wry, black image of my own.

Some times I wondered if I had made Joan up. Other times I
wondered if she would continue to pop in at every crisis of my life
to remind me of what I had been, and what I had been through,
and carry on her own separate but similar crisis under my nose.

Joan's lesbian advances, she perceives, are expressions of the narcissistic
impulses she shares with all the other women who, in patronising Esther,
have tried to make her a projection of their own life-fictions:

My head ached. Why did I attract these weird old women? There
was the famous poet, and Philomena Guinea, and Jay Cee, and
the Christian Science Lady and lord knows who, and they all
wanted to adopt me in some way, and, for the price of their care
and influence, have me resemble them.

Esther, however, keeps Joan at that "cool distance" at which she had always
known her, the "narrative distance" which is Esther's only surety for survival. And if her rebuff in part accounts for Joan's eventual suicide, it is
not something for which Esther can take responsibility. In a sense, she *has*
invented her, but only because Joan chose to identify with that newspaper
image of Esther which Esther herself disclaimed. Structurally, Joan's suicide
and Esther's recovery are arranged in an inverse ratio, to the extent that
Esther is left wondering, at Joan's funeral, just what she thinks she is bury-
ing, the "wry black image" of her madness, or the "beaming double of [her]
old best self." In a sense, the suicide of this surrogate is Esther's rebirth.

The book has abounded in images of ropes and cords and strings of
various kinds that share this ambiguity—the telephone wire which connects
and persecutes, the tramlines of New York, the ECT wires that purify and
burn, the electric chair which kills the Rosenbergs, the rope-tow on the
ski-slopes which offers security at the cost of dependence, the navel-string
which gives life but can strangle. This ambiguity persists into the very last
paragraph, when Esther faces the interviewing committee that is to decide
on her release. The equivocal close opens a new putative future outside the
bell jar of this story:

The eyes and the faces all turned themselves towards me, and
guiding myself by them, as if by a magical thread, I stepped into
the room.

The thread could lead the redeemed heroine out of the "familiar laby-rinth of shovelled asylum paths"; or it could be "the thread that might lead me back to my old, bright salesmanship" spoken of earlier, that makes the puppet dance in the eyes of others. For, if Esther seems at last in control of her own life, she is "guiding [her]self" back on to a public stage, where her future will be decided by the impression she makes on others. The novel closes on a deliberately unresolved upbeat note which never finally clarifies the tension between authentic selfhood and public image, between life as self-articulation and as ritual performance—between, ultimately, "life" itself, and those "attitudes," no matter how deeply assimilated and accredited, which merely counterfeit it.

SANDRA M. GILBERT

"A Fine, White Flying Myth": Confessions of a Plath Addict

Though I never met Sylvia Plath, I can honestly say that I have known her most of my life. To begin with, when I was twelve or thirteen I read an extraordinary story of hers in the "By Our Readers" columns of *Seventeen.* It was called "Den of Lions," and though the plot was fairly conventional, something about the piece affected me in inexplicable, almost "mythic" ways—ways in which I wouldn't have thought I could be affected by a *Seventeen*-reader's story. For one thing, I was faintly sickened by the narrator's oddly intense vision of her experience, an evening spent at a bar with a suave young man and some of his friends. "'Is that a real flower, Marcia?'" asks one of the men in the story, "with [an] oily smile. . . . He had her cornered," thinks Marcia, the protagonist. "No matter what she thought to say, it would be meat for the sacrifice. 'Yes,' she said . . . 'It's real, it's basic.' . . . Basic. The word had been what they wanted. *Toss a slab of raw meat to the lions.* Let them nose it, paw it, gulp it down, and maybe you'll have a chance to climb a tree out of their reach in the meantime."

Could the world really be like this, I wondered. *Was* it like this? How had selves of blood and meat been admitted into the glossily sanitized pages of *Seventeen?* How could anyone so close to my own age (though, thank God, she was significantly older!) have imagined such selves? "Sylvia enjoys being seventeen—'it's the *best* age'" was an editorial comment I found next to another of her contributions. But did she?

Plath next surfaced, of course, as a Guest Editor of *Mademoiselle,* and as winner of that magazine's College Fiction contest—the literary young

From *The Massachussetts Review* 14, no. 3 (Autumn 1978). © 1978 by The Massachusetts Review, Inc.

woman's equivalent of being crowned Miss America. And when I myself became a Guest Editor, four years after she did, I found myself assigned to the same staff editor she had worked for. Now our likenesses, our common problems, as well as our divergences, began to clarify. What I had unconsciously responded to in "Den of Lions," what had made me uneasy about it, was probably that it was a story of female initiation, an account of how one girl learns to see herself as intelligent meat—victim and manipulator of men, costumes, drinks, cigarettes—flesh and artifice together. But what I much more consciously knew about the *Mademoiselle* experience was that for me, as for Sylvia and all the other Guest Editors, it was a kind of initiation ritual, a dramatic induction into that glittery Women's House of fashion and domesticity outside whose windows most of us had spent much of our lives, noses pressed to the glass, yearning to get in, like—to echo Yeats—Keats outside the candy shop of the world.

As *The Bell Jar* suggests, we Guest Editors were on the whole nice, ambitious young women from colleges all over the country. Some of us were interested in fashion, art, and design. But most had won the contest by writing stories or poems or think-pieces about our "Silent Generation," intellectual work that might in other circumstances produce a place on the Dean's List or a Phi Beta Kappa key—an entrance into the spacious male world of work. Instead, because we were all ambivalent about ourselves, cashmere sweater collectors as well as collectors of good grades, we had entered the house of female work, a house, despite all our earlier peering through windows, astonishingly different from what we'd expected.

The magazine offices were pastel, intricately feminine, full of clicking spiky heels. One could almost believe that at midnight they mopped the floors with Chanel No. 5. And almost all the editors and secretaries and assistant editors were career girls—"career gals," I should say—who, as soon as we arrived, began giving us tokens of what we were and where we were, tokens quite unlike those we had become accustomed to at school. Instead of tests or books or grades, for instance, they gave us *clothes*. We sat around in a room that looked like a seminar room, and they wheeled in great racks of college-girl blouses and skirts. Into these we had to fit ourselves, like Cinderella squeezing into the glass slipper. Woe unto you if the blouse doesn't fit, was the message. If the skirt doesn't fit, wear it anyway—at least for the photographer. Later they gave us new hairdos; makeup cases, as in *The Bell Jar;* sheets and bedspreads; dances on starlit rooftops; and more, much more. On those long, hot, June afternoons we sat around in our pastel, air-conditioned seminar room discussing these objects and events as if they were newly discovered Platonic dialogues.

For of course the whole experience of *Mademoiselle* was curiously metaphorical: events occurred, as in a witty fiction, that seemed always to have a meaning beyond themselves. The poisoning in Plath's year, for example, really happened. Yet that doesn't diminish its symbolic significance in *The Bell Jar*. The fashionable menus of Madison Avenue (*Mad* Ave for short) were figuratively as well as literally indigestible. And naturally such unexpected tokens of femininity took their toll among the Guest Editors. Some couldn't bear to go near the "official" residential hotel (which for good reason Plath calls the Amazon). Others became *hysterical*, portentous word, at work or after work. Esther Greenwood, perhaps like Plath herself, throws away her New York clothes, no doubt including all the free "collegiate" outfits.

To complicate things further, for me and for Plath there was the woman Plath calls Jay Cee, the editor with whom we worked every day. Jay Cee was the only woman at the magazine who was not a stereotypical "career gal." Instead, she was a serious, unfashionable, professional woman. But in those ruffly, stylish corridors, she seemed somehow desexed, disturbing, like a warning of what might happen to you if you threw away the clothes and entered the nunnery of art. And like the bald "Disquieting Muses" in an early poem of Plath's, the "dismal-headed / Godmothers" who "stand their vigil in gowns of stone," she constantly forced us to confront ourselves and, additionally, the abyss into which we seemed to be falling. "What are you going to do next?" she would ask. "What are your plans for the future? Have you attempted to publish? Have you thought about a career?" She was efficient; she was kind; she was perfect; yet to a fifties sensibility—suckled by Betty Crocker, weaned on Jayne and Lauren and Marilyn—she seemed, in some mysterious way, terrible.

The next I heard of Sylvia Plath was in the early sixties. She was publishing careful, elegantly crafted poems in places like *The Atlantic* and *The New Yorker*, poems that bore out Robert Lowell's later remarks about her "checks and courtesies," her "maddening docility." Then one day a friend who worked at *The New Yorker* called to say "Imagine, Sylvia Plath is dead." And three days later "Poppies in July," "Edge," "Contusion," and "Kindness" appeared in *TLS*. Astonishingly undocile poems. Poems of despair and death. Poems with their heads in ovens (although the rumor was at first that Plath had died of the flu or pneumonia). Finally the violence seeped in, as if leaking from the poems into the life, or, rather, the death. She had been killed, had killed herself, had murdered her children, a modern Medea. And at last it was really told, the story everyone knows already, and the outlines of history began to thicken to myth. All of us who had read her traced our own journey in hers: from the flashy Women's House of *Mademoiselle* to the dull oven of Madame, from college to villanelles to babies to the scary skeletons of poems we began to study, now, as if they were sacred writ. The Plath Myth, whatever it meant or means, had been launched like a Queen Bee on its dangerous flight through everybody's psyche.

The Plath Myth: is there anything legitimate about such a phrase? Is there really, in other words, an identifiable set of forces which nudge the lives and works of women like Plath into certain apparently mythical (or "archetypal") patterns? In answer, and in justification both of my imagery and of my use of personal material that might otherwise seem irrelevant, I want to suggest that the whole story I have told so far conforms in its outlines to a mythological way of structuring female experience that has been useful to many women writers since the nineteenth century. In Plath's case, the shape of the myth is discernible both in her work and in the life which necessitated that work. In addition, the ways in which as woman and as writer she diverges from the common pattern are as interesting as those ways in which she conforms to it; perhaps, indeed, they will prove more valuable for women writers in the future.

The poet Robert Bly has recently been writing and speaking about the connection between the female psyche and what I am calling the mytho-logical mode. He argues, for instance, that the fairy tale was distinctively a female form, a womanly way of coming to terms with reality, the old matriarchy's disguised but powerful resistance against the encroachments of the patriarchy. While I don't intend, here, to explore all the implications of this assertion, it is obviously related to what I am saying. Women writers, especially when they're writing *as women,* have tended to rely on plots and patterns which suggest the obsessive patterns of myths and fairytales. For instance, what Ellen Moers (writing in *Literary Women*) calls "Female Gothic" is a characteristically mythological genre: it draws heavily upon unconscious imagery, apparently archetypal events, fairytale plots, etc. And, to use Frank Kermode's distinction between myth and fiction, it implies not an "as if" way of seeing the world but a deep faith in its own structures, structures which, to refer briefly to Lévi-Strauss's theory of myth, offer psy-chic solutions to serious social, economic, and sexual-emotional problems. (Male writers, especially since the Romantic period, have also of course worked in this mode, but not with such evident single-mindedness. And male "confessional" poets, like Lowell and Berryman, seem quite able to organize their experience into serious metaphors without it.)

An important question then arises: *why* do so many women writers characteristically work the mythological vein? Some critics might account for the phenomenon—following Bachofen, Neumann, and others—with what I regard as a rather sentimental and certainly stereotypical explanation. The dark, intuitive, Molly Bloomish female unconscious, they'd say, just naturally generates images of archetypal power and intensity.

But it seems to me that a simpler, more sensible explanation might also be possible. Women as a rule, even sophisticated women writers, haven't until quite recently been brought to think of themselves as conscious subjects in the world. Deprived of education, votes, jobs, property rights, they have also, even more significantly, been deprived of their own selfhood. "What shall I do to gratify myself—to be admired—or to vary the tenor of my existence? are not the questions which a woman of right feelings asks on first awaking to the avocations of the day," Mrs. Sara Ellis admonished the Women of England in 1844 [in *The Family Monitor*]. Instead, that energetic duenna of Victorian girls, the Ann Landers of her age, formulated an ideal of ladylike unselfishness—or, better, *selflessness*. "Woman . . . is but a meager item in the catalogue of humanity," she reminded her readers, unless she forgets her "minute disquietudes, her weakness, her sensibility"—in short, unless she forgets her self. So many important men (like Rousseau, Ruskin, and Freud) also expressed this idea that it is no wonder women haven't been able to admit the complex problem of their own subjectivity—their selfhood—either to themselves or others. Rather, they have disguised the stories of their own psychic growth, even from themselves, in a multitude of extravagant, apparently irrelevant forms and images.

For instance, when Charlotte Brontë undertook to write what is essentially a *Bildungsroman*, the story of one young woman's development to maturity, she couldn't write the serious, straightforward, neo-Miltonic account of the "growth of a poet's mind" that Wordsworth produced. A female version of such a narrative would be unprecedented. She couldn't really even use the kind of domestic symbolism Joyce and Lawrence later employed—though attention to domestic detail was said by George Henry Lewes to be a special feminine talent. Instead, she had to sublimate, disguise, mythologize her *rite de passage,* especially in *Jane Eyre* (though also to a lesser extent in *Villette*). This was partly, no doubt, for good commercial reasons. Female Gothic sells, sells now, still, as it sold then. But the main reason, neither inherent nor commercial, was psycho-social. Though Brontë, like many other women, could not think her own inner growth important enough to describe in naturalistic detail, the story itself is of course important: it is *her*story and forces its way out despite the "checks and courtesies" that have folded themselves around her mind, forces its way out in a more conventionally "interesting" and "acceptable" disguise. Thus, in Jane Austen's

novels, other voices, other rooms replace the Wordsworthian egotistical sublime. And in the works of Mary Shelley and the Brontës the most intimate
conflicts of the self with the self, consciously inadmissible, are objectified in
exotic psychodramas—the self splitting, doubling, mythologizing itself until
it hardly seems any longer to have an existence within itself. And in Emily
Dickinson, dressed in white, addressing unread riddles to the world; or Vir-
ginia Woolf, laden with stones, merging with the waters of that dull canal
the river Ouse; or Sylvia Plath, head in a mythic oven—we see the woman
writer herself enacting the psychodrama in life as she had in art, becoming,
as Charles Newman says of Sylvia Plath, the "myth of herself."

So, I would argue, the Plath Myth began with an initiation rite described
in the pages of *Seventeen,* and continued with the induction into the fashionable world of *Mademoiselle* that is examined in *The Bell Jar,* and with the
publication of doggedly symmetrical poems, and the marriage in a foreign
country, and the births of two babies, to the final flight of *Ariel* and the dé-
nouement in the oven and all the rest. And it was of compelling interest to
Plath addicts—indeed, it created Plath addicts—because, like the stories told
by Charlotte Brontë and Mary Shelley, it was figuratively if not literally the
same old story. Disguised, perhaps, but the same. And our own.

But what *was* the story exactly, what were its hidden lineaments, what
was its message? I can best begin to answer this multiple question with
references to a few good critics of Plath's work. Her husband, the poet Ted
Hughes, commented shortly after her death [in *The Art of Sylvia Plath,* ed.
Charles Newman] that "the opposition of a prickly, fastidious defence and
an imminent volcano is, one way or another, an element in all her early
poems." And the words "prickly" and "fastidious" recall Robert Lowell's
remark about "the checks and courtesies" of her "laborious shyness," her
"maddening docility." George Stade, in the best single essay I know about
Plath's work, relates these statements about fastidiousness and docility versus
volcanic intensity to the middle-period poem "In Plaster," a piece in which
the speaker complains that she has been trapped in a tidy but murderous
replica of herself, a plaster cast. "I shall never get out of this!" she exclaims.
"There are two of me now: / This new absolutely white person and the old
yellow one." "The persona speaking out of any given poem by Sylvia Plath,
then," writes Stade

> may be either sulphurous old yellow, or the plaster saint, or a
> consciousness that sometimes contains these two and sometimes
> lies stretched between them. . . . The outer shell of consciousness
> may be completely or dimly aware of the presence within: it may

feel itself a puppet jerked by strings receding into an interior distance where a familiar demon sits in possession, or it may try to locate the menace outside of itself.

Plaster, the outer shell, fastidious defense, checks and courtesies, docility: all these elements clearly fit together in some way. Yet the movement of "In Plaster," as Stade notes, is *out* of the tidiness of plaster, away from the smug perfection of the carved saint, just as the movement of, say, *The Bell Jar* is out of the stale enclosure of the bell jar into a more spacious if dangerous life. And similarly the great poems of *Ariel* often catapult their protagonist or their speaker out of a stultifying enclosure into the violent freedom of the sky. "Now she is flying," Plath writes in "Stings," perhaps the best of the bee-keeping poems,

> More terrible than she ever was, red
> Scar in the sky, red comet
> Over the engine that killed her—
> The mausoleum, the wax house.

And in the title poem of the collection, the one that describes the poet's runaway ride on the horse Ariel, she insists that "I / Am the arrow, / The dew that flies / Suicidal, at one with the drive / Into the red eye, the cauldron of morning." In *The Bell Jar* Plath informs us that Mrs. Willard, the mother of Esther Greenwood's repellent boyfriend, Buddy, believes that "What a man is is an arrow into the future and what a woman is is the place the arrow shoots off from." But, says Esther, "the last thing I wanted was . . . to be the place an arrow shoots off from. I wanted . . . to shoot off in all directions myself, like the colored arrows from a fourth of July rocket."

Being enclosed—in plaster, in a bell jar, a cellar or a waxhouse—and then being liberated from an enclosure by a maddened or suicidal or "hairy and ugly" avatar of the self is, I would contend, at the heart of the myth that we piece together from Plath's poetry, fiction, and life, just as it is at the heart of much other important writing by nineteenth- and twentieth-century women. The story told is invariably a story of being trapped, by society or by the self as an agent of society, and then somehow escaping or trying to escape.

At the beginning of *Jane Eyre*, for instance, Jane is locked into a room— the red room, interestingly, where Mr. Reed, the only "father" she has ever had, "breathed his last": in other words, a kind of patriarchal death chamber, for in this room Mrs. Reed still keeps "divers parchments, her jewel-casket, and a miniature of her dead husband" in a secret drawer in the wardrobe. Panicky, the child stares into a "great looking glass," where her own image looms toward her, alien and disturbing. "All looked colder and darker in that visionary hollow than in reality," the grownup narrator explains. But a mirror, after all, is a sort of box, in which ideas or images of the self are also stored, like "divers parchments." Mirrors, says Sylvia Plath, in a poem called "The Courage of Shutting Up," "are terrible rooms / In which a torture goes on one can only watch." So Jane is doubly enclosed, first in the red room, then in the mirror. Later, of course, it is the first Mrs. Rochester, the raging madwoman, who is closely locked in an attic room, while Jane is apparently free to roam Thornfield at her pleasure. Yet both Jane and the madwoman, it becomes clear, have to escape, whether from actual or metaphorical confinement, Jane by madly fleeing Thornfield after learning of the madwoman's existence, and the madwoman by burning down her prison and killing herself in the process, just as if, curiously, she were an agent not only of her own desires but of Jane's.

Similarly, when we first encounter Sylvia Plath in the macabre contemporary *Bildungsroman* we might as well call *Sylvia Plath*, she is figuratively and later even literally locked into a patriarchal death chamber. "You do not do," she writes at the beginning of "Daddy," in perhaps her most famous lines, "you do not do / Any more, black shoe / In which I have lived like a foot / For thirty years, poor and white, / Barely daring to breathe or achoo." And then, significantly, "Daddy, I have had to kill you."

The enclosure—the confinement—began early, we learn. Though her childhood was free and Edenic, with the vast expanse of Ocean before her (as she tells us in the essay "Ocean 1212-W") when she was nine, "my father died, we moved inland"—moved away from space and playfulness and possibility, moved (if she had not already done so) into the black shoe. "Whereupon," she concludes, "those first nine years of my life sealed themselves off like a ship in a bottle—beautiful, inaccessible, obsolete, a fine, white flying myth." And this is an important but slightly misleading statement, for it was she who was sealed into the bottle, and what she longed for was the lost dream of her own wings. Because, having moved inland, she had moved also into a plaster cast of herself, into a mirror image alien as the image that frightens Jane in the Red Room or the stylish mirrors of the pages of *Mademoiselle,* into the bell jar, into the cellar where she curled like a doped fetus, into the mausoleum, the waxhouse.

In this state, she wrote, "The wingy myths won't tug at us anymore," in a poem in *The Colossus.* And then, in poem after poem, she tried to puzzle out the cause of her confinement. "O what has come over us, my sister! . . . What keyhole have we slipped through, what door has shut?" she asked in

"The Babysitters," a piece addressed to a contemporary. "This mizzle fits me like a sad jacket. How did we make it up to your attic? . . . Lady, what am I doing / With a lung full of dust and a tongue of wood?" she complained in "Leaving Early," a poem written to another woman. And yet again, in a poem called "Dark House," she declared "This is a dark house, very big. . . . It has so many cellars, / Such eelish delvings . . . I must make more maps." For her central problem had become, as it became Jane Eyre's (or Charlotte Brontë's)—how to get out? How to reactivate the myth of a flight so white, so pure, as to be a rebirth into the imagined liberty of childhood?

Jane, and through her Charlotte Brontë, got out, as I suggested, through the mediating madness of the woman in the attic, her enraged crazed double, who burned down the imprisoning house and with it the confining structures of the past. Mary Shelley, costumed as Frankenstein, got out by creating a monster who conveniently burned down domestic cottages and killed friends, children, the whole complex of family relationships. Emily Dickinson, who saw her life as "shaven / And fitted to a frame" (#510), got out by persuading herself that "The soul has moments of Escape— / When bursting all the doors— / She dances like a Bomb, abroad" (#512). Especially in *Ariel*, but also in other works, Plath gets out by (1) killing daddy (who is, after all, indistinguishable from the house or shoe in which she has lived) and (2) flying away disguised as a Queen Bee (in "Stings"), a bear (in the story "The Fifty-ninth Bear"), superman (in the story "The Wishing Box"), a train (in "Getting There" and other poems), an acetylene virgin (in "Fever 103°"), a horse (in "Ariel" and other poems), a risen corpse (in "Lady Lazarus"), an arrow (in "Ariel," *The Bell Jar,* and "The Other"), or a baby (in too many poems to mention).

Of these liberating images or doubles for the self, almost all except the metaphor of the baby are as violent and threatening as Dickinson's bomb, Shelley's monster, or Brontë's madwoman. "I think I am going up. / I think I may rise— / The beads of hot metal fly, and I, love, I / Am a pure acetylene / Virgin," Plath declares in "Fever 103°," ascending "(My selves dissolving, old whore petticoats) / —to Paradise." But not a very pleasant paradise, for this ascent is "the upflight of the murderess into a heaven that loves her," to quote from "The Bee Meeting," and rage strengthens her wings, rips her from the plaster of her old whore life. As the bridegroom, the "Lord of the mirrors," approaches, the infuriated speaker of "Purdah," trapped at his side—"the agonized / Side of green Adam" from which she was born— threatens that "at his next step / I shall unloose . . . From the small jewelled / Doll he guards like a heart . . . The lioness, / The shriek in the bath, / The cloak of holes." "Herr God, Herr Lucifer, / Beware, / Beware," cries Lady

Lazarus. "Out of the ash I rise with my red hair / And I eat men like air." "If I've killed one man, I've killed two—" Plath confesses in "Daddy." "The villagers never liked you. / They are dancing and stamping on you." And in the story "The Fifty-ninth Bear," a tale in which a couple traveling across the western United States on vacation have bet on the number of bears they'll encounter, a great hairy ugly bear lumbers out of the wilderness—and it is the fifty-ninth bear, the wife's bear, for she has chosen the number fifty-nine. First it mauls the woman's silly sunhat, symbol of her whorish domesticity; then violently attacks the husband, who, "*as from a rapidly receding planet,*" (italics mine) hears his wife's wild cry, "whether of terror or triumph he could not tell." But we can tell. We know Sadie, the wife, is dancing like a bomb abroad, like Emily Dickinson or like Sylvia Plath herself. We know we are witnessing "the upflight of the murderess into a heaven that loves her."

Flying, journeying, "getting there," she shrieks her triumph: "The train is dragging itself, it is screaming— / An animal / Insane for the destination . . . The carriages rock, they are cradles. / And I, stepping from this skin / Of old bandages, boredoms, old faces / Step to you from the black car of Lethe, / Pure as a baby." *Pure as a baby!* Skiing suicidally away from "numb, brown, inconsequential" Buddy, Esther Greenwood in *The Bell Jar* plummets down "through year after year of doubleness and smiles and compromise" toward "the pebble at the bottom of the well, the white sweet baby cradled in its mother's belly." *Sweet as a baby!*

How do we reconcile this tender new avatar with the hairy bear, the ferocious virgin, the violent and dangerous Lady Lazarus? That Sylvia Plath wanted to be reborn into the liberty of her own distant childhood—wanted once more to be "running along the hot white beaches" with her father—is certainly true. Yet at the same time, her father represented the leathery house from which she wished to escape. And the baby-images in her poems often seem to have more to do with her own babies than with her own babyhood. In fact, critics often muse perplexedly about the great creative release childbirth and maternity apparently triggered for Plath. And that she loved her children is indisputable—but the fact does not seem any more immediately relevant to an understanding of the self-as-escaping-baby than her longing for her own childhood. Yes, the baby is a blessing, a new beginning— "You're . . . Right, like a well-done sum," says Plath to her child in the poem "You're." Indeed, for the doting mother the baby is even (as in "Nick and the Candlestick") "the one / Solid the spaces lean on, envious," analogous to the redeeming Holy Child, "the baby in the barn." But what have these blessings to do with the monster-mother's liberation? Doesn't the baby, on the contrary, anchor her more firmly into the attic, the dark house, the barn?

The answer to this last question is, I think, *no*—though with some quali-
fications. In fact, for Plath the baby is often a mediating and comparatively
healthy image of freedom (which is another important reason why the Plath
Myth has been of such compelling interest to women), and this is because
in her view the fertile mother is a Queen Bee, an analog for the fertile and
liberated poet, the opposite of that dead drone in the waxhouse who was the
sterile egotistical mistress of darkness and daddy.

We can best understand this polarity by looking first at some poems that
deal specifically with sterility, nullity, *perfection*. "Perfection is terrible, it
cannot have children," Plath wrote in "The Munich Mannequins." "Cold as
snow breath, it tamps the womb / Where the yew trees blow like hydras. . . .
Unloosing their moons, month after month, to no purpose. / The blood flood
is the flood of love / The absolute sacrifice. / It means: no more idols but . . .
me and you." Snow, menstrual blood, egotism, childlessness, the moon, and,
later in the poem, the (significantly) *bald* mannequins themselves, like "orange lollies on silver sticks"—all together these constitute a major cluster of
images which appears and reappears throughout *Ariel* and the other books.
To me they suggest my old, painfully ambivalent vision of the "original" Jay
Cee—Jay Cee the frightening godmother, Jay Cee the disquieting muse—
and I suspect they meant something similar to Plath. "My head ached," says
Esther Greenwood at one point in *The Bell Jar*. "Why did I attract these
weird old women? There was the famous poet and Philomena Guinea and
Jay Cee . . . and they all wanted to adopt me in some way, and . . . have me
resemble them." Bald, figuratively speaking, as "the disquieting muses" of
Plath's poem and De Chirico's painting, these emblems of renunciation were
Plath's—and perhaps every academically talented girl's—earliest "traveling
companions." They counseled "A"s, docility, working for *Mademoiselle,* sur-
rendering sexuality for "perfection," using daddy's old red-leather Thesaurus
to write poems, and living courteously in daddy's shoe, not like a thumbtack,
irascible and piercing, but like a poor white foot, barely daring to breathe or
Achoo.

But "two girls there are," wrote Plath in "Two Sisters of Persephone";
"within the house / One sits; the other, without. / Daylong a duet of shade
and light / Plays between these." The girl within the house, Jay Cee's girl,
"in her dark wainscotted room . . . works problems on / A mathematical
machine," and "at this barren enterprise / Rat-shrewd go her squint eyes."
The other girl, however, "burns open to sun's blade . . . Freely becomes sun's
bride . . . Grows quick with seed" and, "Grass-couched in her labor's pride, /
She bears a king." Or, we might add, a Queen.

The first girl, like the "childless woman" of another poem, sees her "landscape" as "a hand with no lines," her sexuality as "a tree with nowhere to go." The second girl, on the other hand, producing a golden child, produces flight from the folds of her own body, self-transcendence, the dangerous yet triumphant otherness of poetry. For, as Simone de Beauvoir acutely observes in *The Second Sex,* the pregnant woman has the extraordinary experience of being both subject and object at the same time. Even while she is absorbed in her own subjectivity and isolation, she is intensely aware of being an object—a house—for another subject, another being which has its own entirely independent life. Vitality lives in her *and* within her: an ultimate expression of the Shelley-Brontë-Dickinson metaphors of enclosure, doubleness, and escape. "Ordinarily," de Beauvoir remarks, "life is but a condition of existence; in gestation it appears as creative . . . [the pregnant woman] is no longer an object subservient to a subject [a man, a mother, daddy, Jay Cee]; she is no longer a subject afflicted with the anxiety that accompanies liberty; she is one with that equivocal reality: life. Her body is at last her own, since it exists for the child who belongs to her."

That this liberating sense of oneness with life was Plath's predominant attitude toward childbirth and maternity is clear from "Three Women," a verse-play on the subject in which the voice of the First Woman, the healthily golden and achieving mother, is obviously the poet's own, or at least the voice the poet strives to attain. Repudiating yet again the "horrors," the "slighted godmothers" (like the bald muses) "with their hearts that tick and tick, with their satchels of instruments," this speaker resolves to "be a wall and a roof, protecting . . . a sky and a hill of good." For, she exclaims, "a power is growing in me, an old tenacity. / I am breaking apart like the world. . . . I am used. I am drummed into use." Though this passage may sound as if it is about escaping or about writing poetry, it is really about having a baby. And when the child appears later on, he appears in flight—like the escaping virgin, the arrow, or the lioness—a "blue, furious boy, / Shiny and strange, as if he had hurtled from a star" who flies "into the room, a shriek at his heel." And again Plath stresses the likeness of babies, poems, and miraculous escapes: "I see them," she says of babies, "showering like stars on to the world . . . These pure small images. . . . Their footsoles are untouched. They are walkers of air." Living babies, in other words, are escaping shrieks—as poems are; pure small images—as poems are; walkers of air—as poems are: all ways for the self to transcend itself.

Conversely, Plath speaks of dead poems, the poems of jewelled symmetry that would please the disquieting muses, as being like stillborn babies—an analogy which goes back to the male tradition that defines the offspring of "lady poets" as abortions, stillbirth, dead babies. "These poems do not live," she writes in "Stillborn." "It's a sad diagnosis . . . they are dead and their mother near dead with distraction." It becomes clear that certain nineteenth- and twentieth-century women, confronting *confinement* (in both senses of the word) simply translated the traditional baby-poem metaphor quite liter- ally into their own experience of their lives and bodies. "I, the miserable and abandoned, am an *abortion,* to be spurned," said Mary Shelley's monster— and he was, for he escaped from confinement to no positive end. I "step to you from the black car of Lethe / Pure as a baby," cried Plath—meaning, my poems, escaping from the morgue of my body, do that. And "I was in a boundary of wool and painted boards," wrote Anne Sexton. But "we swal- low magic and we *deliver* Anne" ("Third Psalm," in *The Death Notebooks*). For the poet, finally, can be delivered from her own confining self through the metaphor of birth.

Can be, but need not necessarily be. And here we get to the qualifica- tions I mentioned earlier. For while, as de Beauvoir pointed out, the processes of gestation link the pregnant woman with life even as they imply new ways of self-transcendence, they are also frightening, dangerous, and uncontrol- lable. The body works mysteriously, to its own ends, its product veiled like death in unknowable interior darkness. Just as the poet cannot always direct the flow of images but instead finds herself surprised by shocking connec- tions made entirely without the help or approval of the ego, so the mother realizes, as de Beauvoir notes, that "it is beyond her power to influence what in the end will be the true nature of this being who is developing in her womb . . . she is [at times] in dread of giving birth to a defective or a monster." (In other words, in Plath's case, to the ugly bear or the acetylene virgin that she both fears and desires to be.) Moreover, to the extent that pregnancy deper- sonalizes the woman, freeing her from her own ego and instead enslaving her to the species, it draws her backward into her own past (the germplasm she shelters belongs to her parents and ancestors as well as to her) and at the same time catapults her forward into her own future (the germplasm she shelters will belong to her children and their survivors as well as to her). "Caught up in the great cycle of the species, she affirms life in the teeth of time and death," says de Beauvoir. "In this she glimpses immortality; but in her flesh she feels the truth of Hegel's words: 'the birth of children is the death of parents.'" To Plath, this network backwards and forwards was clearly of immense importance. For if having babies (and writing poems) was a way of escaping from the dark house of daddy's shoe, it was also, para- doxically, a frightening re-encounter with daddy: daddy alive, and daddy dead.

Nowhere is that re-vision of daddy more strikingly expressed than in the bee-keeping sequence in *Ariel*. Otto Plath was a distinguished entomologist, author of many papers on insect life, including (significantly) one on "A Muscid Larva of the San Francisco Bay Region Which Sucks the Blood of Nestling Birds." But his most important work was a book called *Bumblebees and Their Ways,* an extraordinarily genial account of the lives of bee colonies, which describes (in passing) the meadows, the nest-boxes, the abandoned cellars inhabited by bumblebees, and the "delicious honey" they make, but concentrates mostly on the sometimes sinister but always charismatic power and fertility of the Queens. The induction of the colony into the bee box, stings, wintering, "the upflight of the murderess into a heaven that loves her"—all these are described at length by Otto Plath, and his daughter must have read his descriptions with intense attention. Her father's red-leather Thesaurus, we're told, was always with her. Why not also *Bumblebees and Their Ways?* Considering all this, and considering also the points made by de Beauvoir, it's almost too fictionally neat to be true that Plath told an interviewer [Douglas Cleverdon in *The Art of Sylvia Plath,* ed. Charles Newman] after the birth of her son, Nicholas, "our local midwife has taught me to keep bees." Yet it is true.

Plath's bee-keeping, at least as it is represented in the *Ariel* sequence, appears to have been a way of coming to terms with her own, female position in the cycle of the species. When the colony is put into the box by "the villagers," *she* is put into "a fashionable white straw Italian hat" (the sort of hat the fifty-ninth bear tears up, the sort of hat they would have given us at *Mademoiselle*) and led "to the shorn grove, the circle of hives." Here she can only imagine the "upflight" of the deadly Queen—for she (both the Queen and the poet), the poem implies, has been put into a box along with the rest of the colony. "Whose is that long white box in the grove, what have they accomplished, why am I cold," she asks. But the question is merely rhetorical, for the box is hers, hers and (we learn in the next poem) perhaps her baby's. "I would say it was the coffin of a midget," she decides there, "or a square baby / Were there not such a din in it." And the rest of the piece expresses the double, interrelated anxieties of poetry and pregnancy: "The box is locked, it is dangerous. I have to live with it . . . I can't keep away from it. . . . I have simply ordered a box of maniacs. They can be sent back. / They can die, I need feed them nothing. I am the owner," culminating in a hopeful resolution: "The box is only temporary."

But when the box is opened, in the third poem, the bees escape like furious wishes, attacking "the great scapegoat," the father whose "efforts" were "a rain / Tugging the world to fruit." And here, most hopefully, the poet, mother of bees and babies, tries to dissociate herself from the self-annihilating stings her box has produced. "*They* thought death was worth it, but I / Have a self to recover, a queen." And "Now she is flying / More terrible than she ever was, red / Scar in the sky, red comet / Over the engine that killed her— / The mausoleum, the waxhouse."

Alas, her flight is terrible because it is not only an escape, it is a death trip. Released from confinement, the fertile and queenly poet must nevertheless catapult back into her dead past, forward into her dead future, like Esther Greenwood plummeting toward the "white sweet baby cradled in its mother's belly," which is, after all, likened to a dead inanimate thing, a still "pebble." "I / Am the arrow, / The dew that flies / Suicidal, at one with the drive / Into the red / Eye, the cauldron of morning," Plath had cried in the poem "Ariel." But just as the fertile poet's re-vision of daddy is killing, so the suicidal cauldron of morning is both an image of rebirth and a place where one is cooked; and the red solar eye, certainly in Freudian terms, is the eye of the father, the patriarchal superego which destroys and devours with a single glance.

A profound and inescapable irony of all the works and lives I've been mentioning is that in her flight from the coffin of herself the woman-writer or the character who is her surrogate is often consumed by the Heraclitean fires of change that propel her forward. Charlotte Brontë's madwoman burns up Rochester's house *and* herself; Mary Shelley's monster plans a funeral pyre to extinguish himself entirely, soul and all; Emily Dickinson's bomb of the spirit will surely explode any minute; and Sylvia Plath, dissolving into the cauldron of morning, "is lost," as she says in the poem "Witch-Burning," "lost in the robes of all this brightness." One may be renewed like a baby in the warm womb of the mythic oven, but the oven is also Auschwitz, Dachau, a place where one is baked like a cookie back into the plaster cast of oneself. Ding Dong the witch is dead: she won't give anybody any trouble any more. The dangers are terrible. Not everyone gets away like Hansel and Gretel.

For this reason, it is the paradox of Plath's life (perhaps of any woman's life) and of the Plath Myth, that even as she longs for the freedom of flight, she fears the risks of freedom—the simultaneous reactivation and disintegration of the past it implies. "What I love is / The piston in motion," Plath says in the poem "Years," then adds ambiguously "My soul *dies* before it." "And you, great Stasis," she continues, "What is so great in that!" Yet at the same time she is drawn to the sea, "that great abeyance"—to the pool of Stasis where the hair of the father spreads in tides like unravelled seaweed. "Father," she had complained in an early poem "this thick air is murderous . . . I would breathe water." And elsewhere, "Stone, stone, ferry me down there," she begged: into the pit, the oven, the sea of stasis, the bottom of the pool where (as she says in "Words") "fixed stars govern a life" and (as she declares in "Edge") "the woman is *perfected*," her children—her independent adulthood—"folded back into her body," "the illusion of a Greek necessity" flowing in "the scrolls of her toga; her bare feet . . . saying, we have come so far, it is over."

What is the way out of this dilemma? How does a woman reconcile the exigencies of the species—her desire for stasis, her sense of her ancestry, her devotion to the house in which she has lived—with the urgencies of her own self? I don't know the answer. For Sylvia Plath, as for many other women, there was apparently, in real life, no way out. But there was a way out in art. And, to honor Sylvia Plath, to honor my addiction to her poems and their place in my own life, I want to stress the positive significance of her art and its optimistically feminine redefinition of traditions that have so far been primarily masculine.

Women and Romantic poets are, after all, alike in certain interesting respects. "Not I, not I, but the wind that blows through me," cried D. H. Lawrence, echoing Wordsworth, Shelley, and a whole Norton Anthology full of others. "A fine wind is blowing the new direction of time" ("The Song of a Man Who Has Come Through"). So, to Plath, when she was working at her best it must have seemed that, as she tells us in *Ariel*, "some god got hold" of her; the processes of body and mind worked their own will, independent of the observing consciousness (which was itself by turns pleased, amused, disgusted, and terrified); cells of thought buzzed and multiplied like bees swarming, or wintering, quiescent; and the babies arrived, Ted Hughes tells us, easily, Frieda, the first, "at exactly sunrise, on the first day of April, the day [Sylvia] regularly marked as the first day of Spring." And so also, and also at sunrise, in (Plath herself noted) "that still blue almost eternal hour before . . . the glassy music of the milkman" [quoted by A. Alvarez in *The Art of Sylvia Plath,* ed. Charles Newman], the "cool morning hours" when Otto Plath wrote that it was best to work and the bees were least "pugnacious," the poems began to arrive, with the strenuous ease of babies—as if the same musing double, the lion-red Queen Bee whom Robert Bly [in *Sleepers Joining Hands*] would call the "ecstatic mother," had liberated them and herself from some Pandora's box. And like the babies, the poems had, now, a squalling imperfection. Where the lines of the earlier "stillborn" works had been stonily symmetrical, jewelled, chiseled, the lines of these later works are long and short, irregular as gasping breath, deliberately imperfect—not because of an impulse to self-indulgence or a failure of control, but because of a conscious decision that "perfection is terrible, it cannot have children."

"The poets I delight in are possessed by their poems as by the rhythms of their own breathing. Their finest poems seem born all of a piece, not put together by hands," Plath wrote toward the end of her life ("Context"). The description applies to her own late poems: possessed of the imperfections of breath, they are nevertheless "born all of a piece," alive, viable, self-sufficient. Out of the waxhouse of *Mademoiselle,* out of the mausoleum of the woman's body, out of the plaster of the past, these poems fly, pure and new as babies. Fly, redeemed—even if their mother was not—into the cauldron of morning.

HUGH KENNER

Sincerity Kills

Very well, the obligatory note of the theatrical. Let's get on with it. Mr. Butscher can help us oblige: "In the new house, off the kitchen, was a windowless room, fairly large, which disturbed Sylvia. . . . Too dark and airless. . . . She felt uneasy when near that room, and her awareness of its existence plagued her sleep. . . . She would later tell her new-found friend, Elizabeth Compton, that she had 'a very eerie feeling that there was another room behind it' and that the room was always there waiting for her."

Elizabeth Compton, you see, remembered that. Sylvia Plath had a life-long knack for saying things people would remember. It entailed sizing up the person, the occasion, as readily as she sized up the consumer of the magazine fiction she also had a knack for. "I just sat there with the whole summer turning sour in my mouth": that's how readers of *Seventeen* like stories to end, as Sylvia very well knew when she was nineteen and fitted "The Perfect Set-Up" with that ending. "I must study the magazines the way I did *Seventeen*," she wrote her mother not long afterward, disclosing plans to "hit *The New Yorker* in poetry and the *Ladies' Home Journal* in stories," and *Letters Home*, where we find that letter, demonstrates, end to end, her thorough mastery of the kind of letter her mother would find gratifying. "Dearest Mother, I am being very naughty and self-pitying in writing you a letter which is very private and which will have no point but the very immediate one of making me feel a little better. Every now and then I feel

From *Sylvia Plath: New Views on the Poetry*, edited by Gary Lane. © 1979 by The Johns Hopkins University Press.

like being 'babied.'" She had studied *Seventeen,* we may want to reflect, the
way she did her mother, for whom she was astute enough to get in there first
with jargon like "self-pity," thus becoming the brave funny girl who's sorry
for herself and knows it and wants her head patted. Esther and her mother
in *The Bell Jar* seem another two people entirely.

If, looking back and forth between Sivvy and Esther, we are so unwise
as to wish to choose the "real" Sylvia Plath, Freud seems to guide us toward
Esther, as though on the principle that hatred of a parent is more apt to
be the authentic emotion. Hatred of "Daddy," too; and hatred of self. But
then Sylvia Plath knew quite well what it was that Freud had denominated
authentic, and even claimed, with remarkable cool, that in "Daddy" she had
merely created a little Freudian monologue. "The poem is spoken by a girl
with an Electra complex. Her father died while she thought he was God.
Her case is complicated by the fact that her father was also a Nazi and her
mother very possibly part Jewish. In the daughter the two strains marry and
paralyze each other—she has to act out the awful little allegory once over
before she is free of it." Just a fictional exercise, in short; by the same token
one might call *Letters Home* an epistolary novel. There's no bottom to this.

Like Aurelia Plath reading Sivvy's letters home, we are continually out-
flanked by someone who knows what we'll approve and how we'll catego-
rize, and is herself ready with the taxonomic words before we can get them
out.

> Daddy, I have had to kill you.
> You died before I had time—

Parlor psychiatry is forestalled; she sketches the complex herself. Lady Lazarus is a bitch? It's not news to *her;* "I eat men like air." (I'm also the only
candid person here.) Our fantasies of anarchic candor stir into life and help
animate *Ariel.* She persuades us that she's daring to say what we wouldn't,
and if we succumb to the spell we're apt to end up believing that *this* is
what we've always wished we could say. That experience isn't good for
anybody, something else she knows. Fans send up a "brute / Amused shout: /
'A miracle!' / That knocks me out"; and fans need reminding that voyeurism
exacts costs:

> There is a charge
>
> For the eyeing of my scars, there is a charge
> For the hearing of my heart—
> It really goes.

And there is a charge, a very large charge,
For a word or a touch
Or a bit of blood

Or a piece of my hair or my clothes.

—As who should say, "The price of absorption in pornography is an incremental deadening of the spirit, an attenuation of an already frail belief in the sanctity of personhood. I shall now show you a pornographic film." All her life, a reader had been someone to manipulate.

To facilitate its understanding with its reader, poetry since Homer's time has had formal ceremonies. It is in this connection that Sylvia Plath herself speaks of manipulation:

> I think my poems come immediately out of the sensuous and emotional experiences I have, but I must say I cannot sympathise with these cries from the heart that are informed by nothing except a needle or a knife or whatever it is. I believe that one should be able to control and manipulate experiences, even the most terrifying—like madness, being tortured, this kind of experience—and one should be able to manipulate these experiences with an informed and intelligent mind. I think that personal experience shouldn't be a kind of shut box and mirror-looking narcissistic experience. I believe it should be generally relevant, to such things as Hiroshima and Dachau, and so on.

These unpremeditated words into a microphone will not be confined to a wholly coherent meaning—how a needle or a knife might inform is unclear, nor whether it's to anyone's advantage if the manipulating intellect connects its own fevers with the Hiroshima fireball—but what she started to say is surely that cries from the heart are not poems until subjected to a discipline like that of her own stanzaic and metrical structures. "Study *The Colossus*," said John Frederick Nims in 1970 [in *The Art of Sylvia Plath,* ed. Charles Newman]. "Notice all the stanza-forms, all the uses of rhythm and rhyme; notice how the images are chosen and related; how deliberately sound is used. It is no accident, for instance, that there are seven identical drab *a*'s in '. . . salt flats, / Gas tanks, factory stacks—that landscape . . .'. Remember that *The Bell Jar* tells us that she 'wrote page after page of villanelles and sonnets,' and this in one semester of one class. Perhaps for writers this is the gist of the Plath case: without the drudgery of *The Colossus*, the triumph of *Ariel* is unthinkable." So let's notice.

Notice the poem about the lady in the stone coffin, sixteen hundred years dead ("All the Dead Dears"). To abridge the discussion, I'll remark that its six stanzas rhyme *abcacb*, one "*b*" line shorter than the norm, the other longer.

> Rigged poker-stiff on her back
> With a granite grin
> This antique museum-cased lady
> Lies, companioned by the gimcrack
> Relics of a mouse and a shrew
> That battened for a day on her ankle-bone.

Stanza 1, and a single audible rhyme: back/gimcrack. It seems an accident in a rhymeless stanza. Stanza 2:

> These three, unmasked now, bear
> Dry witness
> To the gross eating game
> We'd wink at if we didn't hear
> Stars grinding, crumb by crumb,
> Our own grist down to its bony face.

Bear/hear, in the same place, *a/a*, but again as if accidental; it would have been called an eye-rhyme once. Marianne Moore can unsettle in this way, but when Marianne Moore's rhymes fall askew they do so amid a rigorous syllable count. This poem isn't counting syllables. Counting stresses? Perhaps. You can fit the stresses into a 3-2-3-3-3-4 pattern, though with little confidence; "That battened for a day on her ankle-bone" can be read as iambic pentameter, though its partner, "Our own grist down to its bony face," has at most nine syllables, and perhaps five stresses but more likely four. Next stanza:

> How they grip us through thin and thick,
> These barnacle dead!
> This lady here's no kin
> Of mine, yet kin she is: she'll suck
> Blood and whistle my marrow clean
> To prove it. As I think now of her head,

At last an unequivocal rhyme, dead/head, *b/b*; and *a/a* is further off key than before, thick/suck. Which leaves kin/clean; are they *c/c*? In previous stanzas the corresponding words were lady/shrew and game/crumb. The "*c*" rhyme is not proven. And never will be; subsequent stanzas yield in/down, weddings/tang's, go/lie. "*C*" seems a position for—what may we call it?—assonant dissonance.

And in the last stanzas the "*a*" and "*b*" rhymes behave similarly, drifting off into dissonance. In stanza 5 the "*a*" rhymes are as far apart as "they" and "barbecue"; in stanza 4 the "*b*" rhymes are "greatgrandmother" and "hair."

None of which is to assert that poems "ought to" rhyme smartly: simply to notice that between a wholly unfamiliar pattern and a skewing of exemplification, "All the Dead Dears" nearly persuades us that it wasn't rhyming at all, merely striking similar sounds at random. Its mind seems intent on sharp newsmagazine phrases: "Rigged poker-stiff on her back"; "antique museum-cased lady"; "the gross eating game": a smart assurance of diction, O-so-American (she wrote the poem in England; the lady lies "in the Archaeological Museum in Cambridge," where Sylvia Plath was at the time an undergraduate). Stanza 1 and stanza 2 articulate with patness one sentence each.

But the sentence in stanza 3 stops three words into the final line, and when we set out to quote the sentence that offers to fill out the line we find ourselves copying out all the rest of the poem, stanzas 4, 5, 6, unrhymes and all:

As I think now of her head,

From the mercury-backed glass
Mother, grandmother, greatgrandmother
Reach hag hands to haul me in,
And an image looms under the fishpond surface
Where the daft father went down
With orange duck-feet winnowing his hair—

All the long-gone darlings: they
Get back, though, soon,
Soon: be it by wakes, weddings,
Childbirths or a family barbecue:
Any touch, taste, tang's
Fit for those outlaws to ride home on,

And to sanctuary: usurping the armchair
Between tick
And tack of the clock, until we go,
Each skulled-and-crossboned Gulliver
Riddled with ghosts, to lie
Deadlocked with them, taking root as cradles rock.

—as though the poem had suddenly escaped from a sassy phrase-maker's control and commenced spewing out family secrets. Decorum is jettisoned; the daft father's hair, in a zany glimpse, is winnowed by duck-feet. "Darlings" reaches for the throttle; "they / Get back, though, soon, / Soon" asserts cool sarcasm; American diction is given brief rein as outlaws ride home; the final stanza has sweat on its brow. The armchair is a desperate maneuver, so is "skulled-and-crossboned," so is "Gulliver." The whole thing, once it got loose, has just barely been curbed.

That's what the forms in *The Colossus* are often for, to barely assert themselves and get disrupted. They are not like Yeatsian forms, assurances of "traditional sanctity and loveliness"; nor like Marianne Moore forms, assertions that clickety rigor rides what might be impudence; nor like, say, late-Roethke forms, strumming assurances that the balladeer has all this turbulence under control (sort of).

> The Kitty-Cat Bird, he moped and he cried
> Then a real cat came with a Mouth so Wide,
> That the Kitty-Cat Bird just hopped inside;
> "At last I'm myself!"—and he up and he died
> —Did the Kitty—the Kitty-Cat Bird.

That's pretty dreadful, come to think of it, but the verse won't let you think of it right away. Roethke was cunning in effecting such displacements, and Sylvia Plath was fascinated by his craft but never tried to emulate his confident Dada. She's closer, most of the time, to Robert Lowell, who contrived in his earlier work great rickety pseudo-Pindaric formalisms, the point of which is that they are akin only in geometry to seventeenth-century assurances, and later (e.g., "Skunk Hour") approximated as if casually to formalisms whose teasing near presence serves as gauge for nausea. Ted Hughes calls just one poem—"Point Shirley"—a direct Lowell imitation (she wrote it in 1959, while attending Lowell's Boston University seminar), but the similarities pervade her mature work.

Having said that, I'll talk only about Plath, on the understanding that much adjustment of nuance would be entailed in fitting my statements accurately to Lowell. The formalisms of *The Colossus*—assonance, rhyme, stanzaic pattern—serve a number of interdependent offices, one of which is to reassure the genteel reader (and notably the one who counts, the one who edits an upper-middlebrow magazine). This reader wants to see the candles lit and the silver laid out (and so do we, so do we), and will half-accept, half-overlook an intrusion of the mortuary, the morbid, or the demonic provided that table-manners are not disrupted. That first level of sheer calculation should not be discounted; it helps explain how *The New Yorker* came to accept four poems—"Hardcastle Crags," "Man in Black," "Mussel Hunter at Rock Harbor," "Watercolor of Grantchester Meadows"—that scan a scene and come to rest on some deathly emblem capable of disrupting with panic that magazine's normally trite sophistication. "Hardcastle Crags" is especially nightmarish, a journey on foot into fear that keeps inviting us to attend to its compact elegances of phrasing—

> the incessant seethe of grasses
> Riding in the full
>
> Of the moon, manes to the wind,
> Tireless, tied, as a moon-bound sea
> Moves on its root

—so that although clues abound, we barely notice the whole world growing steadily more inimical, stark, unassimilable, with one's death the only appropriate resolution:

> Enough to snuff the quick
> Of her small heat out.

Did any editor notice that the poem's walk was into a cosmic graveyard?

> but before the weight
> Of stones and hills of stones could break
> Her down to mere quartz grit in that stony light
> She turned back.

The wilfully patterned stanzas, the *ababa* off rhymes, effect attention's displacement from perversity to craft.

Perversity? I call it that because, in displacing her own attention too, she indulges herself in reconstructing that walk with lurid specificity, forcing a stated unmeaning into its landscape, transforming a mood into something like an article of belief.

> All the night gave her, in return
> For the paltry gift of her bulk and the beat
> Of her heart was the humped indifferent iron
> Of its hills, and its pastures bordered by black stone set
> On black stone.

Living with the poem, working out its nine stanzas, fifty-four lines, retouching its ingenious assonances (*struck/* street/ *black/* ignite/ *shake*) and the riding of its sentences over stanza breaks (these coincide only once, at the end of stanza 5), she could, telling herself she was solving technical puzzles, pencil taboo combinations into its grid, almost as the rhyme of a limerick gives one license to utter a scatology, and rise from her work perhaps incrementally more convinced than before that Sivvy and the huge physical world were incompatible.

I don't want to melodramatize this; but it's been contrived that the manner of her death cannot but haunt any discussion of her work, and read in that knowledge the poems of *The Colossus* offer us the spectacle of someone accustoming herself to the necessity of a speedy death: the more so the longer, clearly, they took to write (thesaurus on lap, Ted Hughes tells us, for all the world as though nothing of more moment were going forward than the completion of the day's crossword puzzle). Here off-rhymes are especially betraying. Since they won't serve as finding devices for one another the way "bright" prompts "light," they entail a search and trial that must linger and brood; that can choose, as if uncoerced, to call the hills "humped indifferent iron," yet justify "iron" by the need of an assonance for "return." So, poem by poem, the universe was fitted with a bleak vocabulary, freely chosen yet seemingly necessary.

By the time her poetic had gone into free fall—Ted Hughes dates this from "The Stones," the last poem in the Knopf *Colossus*—that vocabulary came at call: stones, iron, bleak light, all solid things inimical, all gentle locutions used bitterly ("My swaddled legs and arms smell sweet as rubber" and "There is nothing to do. / I shall be good as new.").

> There is nothing to do.
> I shall be good as new.

That's not an off-rhyme nor a dissonant assonance. It's a vibration on target, shrieking its mocking echo of psychiatric reassurance. It's also the rhyme sound of "Daddy."

Here and there, in *The Colossus,* we can detect her working back toward interdicted material: as when "All the Dead Dears" sidles from the innocuous Baedeker note about something you can see in the Archaeological Museum in Cambridge (nothing wrong, is there, with staring at an educational exhibit?) past two stanzas of brisk description to a sudden unmasking of family skeletons: "Mother, grandmother, greatgrandmother / Reach hag hands to haul me in" and "daft father" looms "under the fishpond surface" beneath which he has long ago been drawn; and they won't stay dead, and they claim us, keep us "deadlocked." "The Stones," the first free-fall poem, need not sidle; it installs itself at a bound in the madhouse of six years before:

This is the city where men are mended.
I lie on a great anvil.

and

The grafters are cheerful,

Heating the pincers, hoisting the delicate hammers.
A current agitates the wires
Volt upon volt. Catgut stitches my fissures.

The unpardonable insult, electroshock therapy. Borrowing a melodramatic image from her, we can say that she has opened the eerie waiting room she told Elizabeth Compton about and stepped into a lurid past. Or we can say that when furies lurk just beyond the rim of consciousness there is paramount danger in improvising. All the formal defenses are down.

For that had been a final use of the intricate formalisms: they detained her mind upon the plane of craft, and so long as it was detained there it did not slip toward what beckoned it. Working on the plane of craft, it made some very good poems indeed, which the vertigo of *Ariel* has since persuaded readers to call contrived, frigid, academic. That seems a doubly erroneous judgment. If we think of *The Colossus* not as the frigid precursor to *Ariel* but as the work of a very intelligent girl in her mid twenties, it is an amazingly good collection. There is no guessing how far in ten more years she might have developed that way of working. It is a plausible guess that the arc of her development might have easily exceeded Lowell's. That rich resourcefulness of diction, that command of craft, that intentness—it is hard to think of a first collection that promises so much. And the other error that adheres in our easy preference for *Ariel* is its overlooking of the fact that as long as she worked in the manner of *The Colossus* she kept safely alive. One prefers one's poets kept alive.

But no, *Ariel* has been made to seem a new and final sincerity. Ted Hughes gives conventional opinion its cue: until "The Stones," at Yaddo, he writes [in *The Art of Sylvia Plath,* ed. Charles Newman], "she had never in her life improvised. The powers that compelled her to write so slowly had always been stronger than she was. But quite suddenly she found herself free to let herself drop, rather than inch over bridges of concepts." Note the loaded terms: with "The Stones," which I would call her first sick poem, she had overcome the compulsion of inhibiting powers. She is "free" (to drop). And she inches no longer. Inching is an ignoble mode of progress, is it not? Never mind that Milton inched. Hughes goes on: in her final phase she "was able to turn to her advantage all the forces of a highly-disciplined, highly intellectual style of education which had, up to this point, worked mainly against her, but without which she could hardly have gone so coolly into the regions she now entered." What she did now was write "at top speed, as one might write an urgent letter. From then on, all her poems were written in this way."

What had, in Ted Hughes's phrase, "worked mainly against her" was a set of habits that, if I read aright, had kept her producing and alive. I would not blame those habits for the frigidities and immaturities of *The Colossus:* I would guess that she was late to mature, and frigid. The strident insincerities of even the later *Letters Home* may help us gauge how much of her mind was still taken up with role playing; will power and ambition incited, habits of craftsmanship released, extraordinary poems from the part of her talent that could be mobilized nonetheless.

> From Water-Tower Hill to the brick prison
> The shingle booms, bickering under
> The sea's collapse.
> Snowcakes break and welter.
>
> ("Point Shirley")

Poets have imitated the sea's sound since Homer, never more authoritatively than in such a detail as this. Alert fidelity to the actual produced the *clou*-word, "bickering," with its aural reminiscence of "brick" and its fine antithetical play against "booms," before "sea's collapse" terminates the wave in a hiss of sibilants. She used less of her talent in better-known lines:

> Dying
> Is an art, like everything else.
> I do it exceptionally well.
>
> I do it so it feels like hell.
> I do it so it feels real.
> I guess you could say I've a call.

I find nothing to alter in the way I described [in "Ariel—Pop Sincerity"] the more lurid parts of *Ariel* the year it was published:

> Sparse rhymes come and go nearly at random, and the number
> of syllables in a line swings with the vertigo of her thought. Still,
> these are shaped poems, all but two of them measured out in
> stanzas, by preference with an odd number of lines (5 or 3).
> Not that they resemble in the least Villon's ceremonious ballades.

Perhaps some of them only play the desperate game of repeating again and again the stanza the opening fell into; there's more of compulsion neurosis than mathematics in those forms; the breaks between stanzas are like cracks in the sidewalk, on which she is careful never to step.

The resulting control, sometimes *look* of control, is a rhetoric, as cunning in its power over our nerves as the stream of repulsions. It in fact enacts its own inability to govern. Naked negation spilling down the sides of improvised vessels, that is the formal drama of poem after poem. Being formal, it saves them from shrillness.

The negation, liquid, labile, repudiates with the gleeful craft of a mad child other persons, the poet's own body, the entire created universe. . . .

> Only let down the veil, the veil, the veil.
> If it were death
>
> I would admire the deep gravity of it, its timeless eyes.
> I would know you were serious.
>
> There would be a nobility then, there would be a birthday.
> And the knife not carve, but enter
>
> Pure and clean as the cry of a baby,
> And the universe slide from my side.

This is insidious nausea; Robert Lowell writes in his Foreword of the serpent he hears whispering from her lines, "Come, if you only had the courage, you too could have my rightness, audacity and ease of inspiration." But most of us, he adds, will turn back: "These poems are playing Russian roulette with six cartridges in the cylinder."

Poems like "A Birthday Present," from which that last quotation comes, have a Guignol fascination, like executions. She was somewhere on the far side of sanity, teasing herself with the thrill of courting extinction, as though on a high window ledge. Such spectacles gather crowds and win plaudits for "honesty" from critics who should know better. In those terrible months the habits of craft lasted, a feel for shaping and phrasing gone into her bones. Rhyme, though, was no longer a diffraction grating but a wild heuristic, prompting, encouraging—

> You do not do, you do not do
> Any more, black shoe.

She could have done without that voodoo encouragement. It's too much to say the poems killed her, but one can't see that they did anything to keep her alive. The death poems—say a third of *Ariel*—are bad for anyone's soul. They give a look of literary respectability to voyeurist passions: no gain for poetry, nor for her.

True Plath fans will detest all of the foregoing. True Plath fans, when articulate, are busy making points about purity and sincerity: in quest (I find I wrote eleven years ago) "of spiritual shortcuts to spiritual virtues, but preferring to see someone else try them out." The true self into which Sylvia Plath's soul merged when her careful habits of composition failed her—the habits Ted Hughes stigmatizes as having "worked mainly against her"—made a virtue of a Manichaean lack of patience with the world's slow turning. The world, its obduracy, respect for the waves and stones of which had once summoned all her craft, came to mean only minatory forms, the yew tree whose message "is blackness—blackness and silence," and the body's "aguey tendon, the sin, the sin." In fever, pulsating at a distance from the world,

> I
>
> Am a pure acetylene
> Virgin
> Attended by roses.

This is bogus spirituality, and it has its admirers, who even seem pleased that Sylvia Plath did not survive it.

J. D. McCLATCHY

Short Circuits and Folding Mirrors

Read together, Aurelia Schober Plath's edition of her daughter's *Letters Home* and Edward Butscher's overheated, undiscriminating, yet interesting biography, *Sylvia Plath: Method and Madness,* remind one of the strong "period" quality of this poet's life and attitudes. McCarthyism, heavy petting, the military-industrial complex, *The New Yorker,* bomb shelters, the vocationalism and domesticity, the unfocused neuroses and emotional hyperbole—these suggest the era: Plath's ambitions and anxieties were redolent of the ruthless vanities and sad defenses of Eisenhower's America. Even the most extensive and convincing interpretations of Plath's work—Judith Kroll's elaborate, even pedantic *Chapters in a Mythology: The Poetry of Sylvia Plath*—reinforces this sense by reading the career in terms of the then fashionable murk of Robert Graves's White Goddess mythologies. In Plath's "mythicized biography," Kroll contends, the poet's confessional impulses were subsumed by archetypal patterns and strategies that at once revealed, organized, and articulated her experience in poetry. In impressive detail, Kroll traces through Plath's sources and imagery the poet's pursuit of the Muse as both the subject of her work and its inspiration. There is no doubt that Plath resorted to and exploited various back-of-the-brain protocols as a ready-made source of images and plots that, at the same time, were resonant with and focused the facts of her own life.

Kroll's is a symptomatic response to this poet, though more intelligent than most. The establishment of a cult, with accompanying distortions of attention, inflated claims, and rapt explications, normally attends the appear-

From *Sylvia Plath: New Views on the Poetry,* edited by Gary Lane. © 1979 by The Johns Hopkins University Press.

ance and aftermath of any "period" poet. (I do not mean that as a pejorative term; among others, Shelley and Arnold, Hart Crane and Frank O'Hara seem to me equally "period" poets, whose sensibilities uniquely captured—and whose work continues to recover for later readers—their contemporary culture's tone, values, and issues.) I suspect that, in retrospect, Plath will have emerged as the most distinctly "period" poet of her generation. Already she is viewed as a cultural, as well as a literary, phenomenon. Alternately heroine or victim, martyr or scapegoat, she has been symbolized and exploited so hauntingly in the cultural consciousness that it is difficult not to read her life—with its gestures of defiance, compulsion, and despair—rather than her work, in which those gestures are reflected or reimagined. But Plath is also an especially representative figure of the directions and dynamics of poetry in the early 1960s. And I think that can be seen nowhere more clearly than in a stylistic reading of her work, of the ways in which she absorbed and altered the poetic climate then prevailing. In the dedicatory poem to *Nones,* which was published at about the time Plath first began writing verse, Auden caught the official tone exactly when he spoke of a "civil style" vitiated by "the wry, the sotto-voce, / Ironic and monochrome." Her initiation into such a situation, her attempts to master it while achieving an individual voice, the methods she used to dismantle or energize such a polite inheritance, and her shift to a more daringly expressionistic and highly inflected verse—all of these are aspects of a larger trend then occurring in poetry. But in a poignantly foreshortened way, Plath got there first, so that her career remains paradigmatic. Its force and permanence reside less in her subjects than in her rapidly evolving relationship to style, and in her final accomplishment of a form that combines its prosody, imagery, and tone with a unique and abiding authority.

Plath was an assiduous apprentice, and put herself resolutely through the traditionalist paces and patterns. However predictably feeble or vapid the results were, she did acquire a degree of technical expertise and fluency, so that by the time she considered herself a professional she had ready answers to an interviewer's [Lee Anderson's] question about her sense of craft:

> Technically I like it to be extremely musical and lyrical, with a singing sound. I don't like poetry that just throws itself away in prose. I think there should be a kind of constriction and tension which is never artificial yet keeps in the meaning in a kind of music too. And again, I like the idea of managing to get wit in with the idea of seriousness, and contrasts, ironies, and I like visual images, and I like just good mouthfuls of sound which

have meaning. . . . At first I started in strict forms—it's the easiest way for a beginner to get music ready-made, but I think that now I like to work in forms that are strict but their strictness isn't uncomfortable. I lean very strongly toward forms that are, I suppose, quite rigid in comparison certainly to free verse. I'm much happier when I know that all my sounds are echoing in different ways throughout the poem.

What is curious in that hurried litany of modernist pieties is that her attention was as often fixed on the possibility of error as of achievement. And indeed, her early poetry consistently pursues and portrays her abilities rather than her experience; in fact, that is frequently the explicit subject of the poems themselves: "Hardcastle Crags," "The Ghost's Leavetaking," "Black Rook in Rainy Weather," "A Winter Ship," "Ouija," "Snakecharmer," "Moonrise," and the uncollected "On the Difficulty of Conjuring Up a Dryad." These are all poems that worry the difficulty of aligning reality and vision, and "vision" in *The Colossus* is a term with no mystical force. It is Plath's word for art itself—a transcendent, idealized heterocosm, ordered and self-reflexive. It is, in other words, the well-wrought poetics of the modernist masters and their New Critics: Yeats, Stevens, and Auden, as domesticated and institutionalized by Brooks-and-Warren. *The Colossus* is not merely the poetry of an ambitious but cautious beginner; it is a summary of the prevalent mode, and Plath's imagination, though equal to its forms and discretions, was not yet strong enough to assert a personality apart from the mimed voice. She followed the rules of the game, and generally set low stakes.

Her first collection betrays the novice's self-consciousness. It is a poetry of chosen words, of careful schemes and accumulated effects; its voice is unsteady, made up. It leans heavily on its models and sources; there are broad hints of help from Stevens, Roethke, even Eliot. The refinement of this poetry derives not only from its being influenced or allusive. There is also a kind of awkward delicacy to it—which may come from her identification of herself with what she thought was a genteel line of women poets like Marianne Moore or Elizabeth Bishop, or may be connected with her insistent academicism. Whatever the reasons, there is an inhibited quality to the verse's perspectives, as well as a distinctly literary cast to many of the poems that borrow Oedipus or Gulliver, Byron or Medea, Gabriel or Lucine for their authority. Another symptom is the stiff, stale diction that rattles around in so many of these poems: words like "cuirass," "wraith," "descant," "bole," "bruit," "casque," "ichor," "pellicle." This is a language found nowadays only in the columns of a Thesaurus—an underlined copy of which Ted Hughes remembers always on his wife's knee at the time, as if she were more interested in the unusual than in the appropriate word. One need only compare her "Sow" to "View of a Pig" by Hughes—who early became and always remained the strongest influence on her work—to sense the more natural ease with which he urges and controls his language and the power it draws from strangeness. His dead pig retains a menacing vitality, as Hughes narrows his regard, pares his description, and concentrates on essentials. Plath, on the other hand, fusses with piggy banks and parslied sucklings, a constantly shifting metric, long sentences, and a glut of adjectives—all of which dilute her argument and blur the poem's occasion and subject.

In 1958, at a time when she was as devoted to drawing as she was to verse, Plath wrote to her mother, "I've discovered my deepest source of inspiration, which is art"—not an unusual discovery for any young poet. But she was not referring only to the origins of poems, though she drew on Breughel's *The Triumph of Death,* Rousseau's *Charmeuse de Serpents,* and De Chirico's *The Disquieting Muses,* among others. I take her to have meant her method as well. It is not merely those expected *Gemäldegedichte* that would lead one to call most of the poems in this book *compositions.* Throughout, she is attracted to textures and shapes, to landscape, primary colors and gradated shades, grounded figures, and above all, to design. These are, of course, concerns and effects that enact the then dominant aesthetic, with its stress on correctness and perspicuity, on elaborated forms, on the observing eye and ordering mind.

The pictorial bias in *The Colossus* has, in turn, inevitable stylistic consequences. "Man in Black" is a convenient example:

> Where the three magenta
> Breakwaters take the shove
> And suck of the grey sea
>
> To the left, and the wave
> Unfists against the dun
> Barb-wired headland of
>
> The Deer Island prison
> With its trim piggeries,
> Hen huts and cattle green
>
> To the right, and March ice
> Glazes the rock pools yet,
> Snuff-coloured sand cliffs rise

Over a great stone spit
Bared by each falling tide,
And you, across those white

Stones, strode out in your dead
Black coat, black shoes, and your
Black hair till there you stood,

Fixed vortex on the far
Tip, riveting stones, air,
All of it, together.

The poem is in the rhyme scheme that most frequently appears in Plath's early poetry, slanted terza rima. (It seems typical of this poet that she favored one of the most stylized and difficult verse forms in English, and then worked against its strictures. It is as if she wanted to take advantage of a tradition, but without ever seeming to do so.) The entire poem—and this is unusual for Plath—consists of just one long sentence. The careful, pointed exposition is clearly blocked in hard edges, not unlike those drawings by Plath I have seen that are heavy, dark, flat. This poem's "narrative" has preceded the opening stanza, its one character is outline and absence, and all its details converge toward the last, abstract stanza (which seems to echo Wordsworth), where the mysterious human figure alone establishes the relationships among the objects that, in random ensemble, comprise the scene. It is, in other words, a poem about the poet; a poem about itself, its single sentence containing the whole. But notice too that each of its shifts of direction or attention is signaled by "and." This is a characteristic of Plath's early poems—this, or her constant use of an appositional format, usually a metaphor per line. Such tactics count on a *succession* of ideas, objects, or equivalents to structure a poem, and not on their *interdependence*, relationships that a more complex syntax, for instance, would demonstrate. Plath's technique tends to give the same lexical value to the different parts of the poem, and thus produces a flattening or equalizing effect—like a painting with no perspective.

Instead of animating her poems by the intricacies of arrangement, she tries to invest them with a kind of verbal and metrical energy, almost as if to distract the reader from their meanings, to veil their deeper significance of subject and flourish instead their versified foreground. Levels of diction, from the colloquial to the exalted, are inexcusably jumbled. Parts of speech are regularly interchanged, forceful predicative words are especially favored as substitutes. And though rhyme schemes (or, occasionally, syllabics) are employed to steady a stanza, the metric of any one line within that stanza is erratic and aggressive. Accents may be syncopated, but most often are just heaped up. Plath does the same thing with adjectives, which abound. The combination results in a blistered, hectoring line that lacks any real subtlety or persuasion. She doesn't like to play on or with words; she rarely uses enjambments successfully or ingeniously. She is concerned, then, primarily with the length, the intensity, and the patterning of her lines and poems, and not with their modulation or variety.

Ted Hughes thinks that most of Plath's early poems turn on "the opposition of a prickly, fastidious defence and an imminent volcano"—an antagonism, finally, between the disciplines of her art and the demands of her experience. "Poem for a Birthday," the sequence that concludes the British edition of *The Colossus,* seems her first calculated effort to discover rather than impose the form of her experience. Despite its reliance on Roethke, there is a new assurance and freedom to the verse that permits strong tonal effects and interesting elliptical cuts. Perhaps that is because these poems are not dominated by the representational eye but by the presentational vagaries of the unconscious. Again, I suspect the influence of Hughes. It was at about this time that he turned her attention away from studying poetry toward mystical and anthropological texts; away from formal literary exercises and more seriously toward horoscopes, the tarot, the ouija board, improvisations, meditational devices, and free association games. In its own way, each is a ritualistic yet unstructured procedure to release experience from the unconscious, to which one would give voice rather than shape. This corresponds with Plath's own sense of poetic strength, which was invariably bound up with the notion and sensation of release. After the birth of her two children, she began to write with an increasingly confident maturity, just as later her separation from her husband delivered her into a final creative fury—Judith Kroll notes that in October 1962, the month after her separation, she wrote at least twenty-six poems. *The Bell Jar* seems to have had a kind of purgative function for its author, and her simultaneous discovery of the confessional poetry of Robert Lowell and Anne Sexton—which provided her the necessary examples of how to include her life in poetry—she also described in terms of release.

Each is a release *into* the self, into emotional and psychological depths either cultivated by or thrust upon her. And at the same time, she was prompted to free her work of the inhibitions, both psychological and stylistic, that had restricted her first book. It is very difficult to analyze in clear, progressive detail a stylistic "development" such as Plath's, which matured in only a few years and could change radically over several months. (And the situation is further complicated by the incomplete and confusing editions of her work.) Still, her so-called "transitional" collection, *Crossing the Water,* can be read as a record of her experiments to secure the rapid advances she made over *The Colossus.* Take, for instance, the opening stanza of "Finisterre":

> This was the land's end: the last fingers, knuckled and rheumatic,
> Cramped on nothing. Black
> Admonitory cliffs, and the sea exploding
> With no bottom, or anything on the other side of it,
> Whitened by the faces of the drowned.
> Now it is only gloomy, a dump of rocks—
> Leftover soldiers from old, messy wars.
> The sea cannons into their ear, but they don't budge.
> Other rocks hide their grudges under the water.

Plath's use of a word like "cannons" is familiar enough, but those rocks that "hide their grudges under the water" are new; they mark a shift from the striking word to the startling image. And furthermore, this is an image whose occasion and impact are calculated, controlled, and coaxed from the opening line's clutching hand of land. The poem's effects, in other words, are less immediate and transient. The brace of a rhyme scheme is gone, and the lines are irregular in length. Both those decisions seem a part of Plath's desire to approximate the rhythms of speech. Her poetry is never exactly conversational, but "Finisterre," if not the "direct, even plain speech" that Hughes says she was soon striving for in an effort to escape the rhetoric of the official High Style, has at least the effect of a soliloquy's heightened naturalism—an effect that her radio script "Three Women" displays brilliantly, though it comes at the expense of the theatrical. In her last work, Plath intensified that voice, but it always remained a dialogue between the mind and itself.

Although several of the "transitional" poems—say, "The Babysitters" or "In Plaster"—are too prosaic, they are merely the failures of Plath's otherwise successful project to give her poems a more dramatic posture, not merely by manipulating a poem's rhythms and imagistic resources, but by providing a situation for its voice. "Face Lift" and "Parliament Hill Fields" are fine examples of Plath's new awareness of plotting a poem, implying a character—of accumulating significance within the poem's own narrative. It was a necessary step toward the refracted events and mysterious presences in *Winter Trees* and *Ariel.* What, in the late poetry, seems blurred by psychic disjunctiveness is given its force by the hard exactness of tone, and the poems in *Winter Trees*—poems like "Purdah," "Childless Woman," "By Candlelight," and "Thalidomide"—have a heightened, penetrating force that her poems of mid passage lack. There is something more than the psychological realism of accommodating narrated facts into poetry, or of using the poem itself to discover her experiences rather than merely to record or fantasize her feelings about them. By the time one reads *Winter Trees*, one hears a voice grown markedly more inflected—usually with an angry irony:

> O maiden aunt, you have come to call.
> Do step into the hall!
> With your bold
> Gecko, the little flick!
> All cogs, weird sparkle and every cog solid gold.
> And I in slippers and housedress with no lipstick!
>
> ("The Tour")

And the tone of voice comes increasingly to determine the line breaks, now a collusion of image and breath:

> Do not think I don't notice your curtain—
> Midnight, four o'clock,
> Lit (you are reading),
> Tarting with the drafts that pass,
> Little whore tongue,
> Chenille beckoner,
> Beckoning my words in—
> The zoo yowl, the mad soft
> Mirror talk you love to catch me at.
>
> ("Eavesdropper")

Increasingly in her later work, as here, the voice becomes both the rhythmical principle and the context for meaning. In poems like "By Candlelight" or "The Other" the syntax of accusation or inquiry or reaction, the disjunctive details of private experience, and the spliced images of her surrealist tendencies, begin to merge into what can be called a characteristic poem. In *Crossing the Water,* for example, "Last Words" or "A Life" still display the tension of the will doing the work of the imagination. But in a later poem like "The Other," the willfulness yields to a purified, demonic energy, an insistent inevitability:

> You come in late, wiping your lips.
> What did I leave untouched on the doorstep—
>
> White Nike,
> Streaming between my walls!

Smilingly, blue lightning
Assumes, like a meathook, the burden of his parts.

The police love you, you confess everything.
Bright hair, shoe-black, old plastic,

Is my life so intriguing?
Is it for this you widen your eye-rings?

One way to approach and appreciate the stylistic breakthrough of *Ariel* is to trace some of the recurrences of a single concern—her father, The Father—to its treatment in the book's most famous poem, "Daddy." The plain-prose version is in *The Bell Jar,* whose narrator, Esther Greenwood, "was only purely happy until [she] was nine years old," when her father— who had come "from some manic-depressive hamlet in the black heart of Prussia"—had died. And Esther, on the psychotic verge of suicide, "had a great yearning, lately, to pay [her] father back for all the years of neglect, and start tending his grave." It is only a simple sense of loss, of the horrible distance between the living and dead, that is revealed:

> At the foot of the stone I arranged the rainy armful of azaleas I had picked from a bush at the gateway of the graveyard. Then my legs folded under me, and I sat down in the sopping grass. I couldn't understand why I was crying so hard.
> Then I remembered that I had never cried for my father's death.
> My mother hadn't cried either. She had just smiled and said what a merciful thing it was for him he had died, because if he had lived he would have been crippled and an invalid for life, and he couldn't have stood that, he would rather have died than had that happen.
> I laid my face to the smooth face of the marble and howled my loss into the cold salt rain.

Immediately after this scene, Esther returns from the graveyard, swallows the pills, hides in a cellar hole, and lies down to death: "The silence drew off, baring the pebbles and shells and all the tatty wreckage of my life. Then, at the rim of vision, it gathered itself, and in one sweeping tide, rushed me to sleep." Given the point of view, the emotion here is left distanced and unaccountable, and is told with the restraint that Plath uses throughout the novel to draw out slowly its cumulative effects of disorientation and waste. But the images of stone and sea, sleep and escape, quarry and fear, that structure her account are important. In a memoir written for a 1963 broadcast, "Ocean 1212-W," Plath broods on her relationship with the sea

and her earliest self: the miracles of immersion and completion. The birth
of her younger brother then defined for her, of her, "the *separateness* of
everything. I felt the wall of my skin: I am I. That stone is a stone. My
beautiful fusion with the things of this world was over. The tide ebbed,
sucked back into itself." And later, at the end: "My father died, we moved
inland. Whereon those nine first years of my life sealed themselves off like a
ship in a bottle—beautiful, inaccessible, obsolete, a fine, white flying myth."

To watch this myth, these images, resumed in the poems discovers Plath,
at first, refining and deepening her metaphor with the precisions of verse.
In "The Colossus," the girl clambers in helpless self-absorption over the
mammoth ruins of her father:

> Thirty years now I have laboured
> To dredge the silt from your throat.
> I am none the wiser.
>
> Scaling little ladders with gluepots and pails of lysol
> I crawl like an ant in mourning
> Over the weedy acres of your brow
> To mend the immense skull-plates and clear
> The bald, white tumuli of your eyes.
>
> A blue sky out of the Oresteia
> Arches above us.

The figure is right: its immense size symbolizing her incest-awe, its ruined
fragments projecting her ambivalent feelings. But the mystery of loss and
betrayal, the secretive sexual fantasies, the distortions of knowledge and
memory, are left unexplored, dependent solely on the poem's figurative force:

> Nights, I squat in the cornucopia
> Of your left ear, out of the wind,
> Counting the red stars and those of plum-colour.
> The sun rises under the pillar of your tongue.
> My hours are married to shadow.
> No longer do I listen for the scrape of a keel
> On the blank stones of the landing.

It is *The Bell Jar*'s suicidal darkness she curls into here, longing to be reborn
into return; it is the same sea that threatens suitors. The same sea that washes
through "Full Fathom Five": "Your shelled bed I remember. / Father, this
thick air is murderous. / I would breathe water." The same stone in "The
Beekeeper's Daughter," a poem addressed to "Father, bridegroom": "My

heart under your foot, sister of a stone." The same dark exclusion that ends "Electra on Azalea Path":

> I am the ghost of an infamous suicide,
> My own blue razor rusting at my throat.
> O pardon the one who knocks for pardon at
> Your gate, father—your hound-bitch, daughter, friend.
> It was my love that did us both to death.

In all of these early poems, the images are retried to approximate the experience, but their equivalents cannot manage its depth and intricacies. But "Daddy"—the title alone indicates that she will write out of the experience directly—is suddenly, strikingly different, even as its details are finally aligned. The echoes we are meant to recall sound with a first force: "black shoe / In which I have lived like a foot / For thirty years, . . . Marble-heavy, a bag full of God, / Ghastly statue, . . . a head in the freakish Atlantic." The language and movement of "Daddy" are entirely new: instead of slow, careful gestures, the poem races its thickly layered and rhymed syncopation into some strange, private charm to evoke and exorcise a demon-lover. The short lines—which Plath reads with tremulous contempt in her recording of the poem—have a formulaic quality appropriate to the murderous ritual that the poem enacts: "Daddy, I have had to kill you. / You died before I had time." But what is most extraordinary about this poem is the amount and complexity of experience that it can convincingly include. If "The Colossus" deals with remorse, "Daddy" deals in guilt. The poem veers between love and hate, revenge and regret, Eros and Thanatos. Imagining herself as a Jew and her father as a Nazi, or her husband as a vampire and herself as a maiden, the poet languishes in the need for punishment to counter the loss of love. The ambivalence of identification and fear is used to reveal more than "The Colossus" even hints at:

> Every woman adores a Fascist,
> The boot in the face, the brute
> Brute heart of a brute like you.
>
> . . . .
>
> At twenty I tried to die
> And get back, back, back to you.
> I thought even the bones would do.
>
> But they pulled me out of the sack,
> And they stuck me together with glue.
> And then I knew what to do.

> I made a model of you,
> A man in black with a Meinkampf look
>
> And a love of the rack and the screw.
> And I said I do, I do.

The paranoid's identification of the persecutor with the rejected father, the macabre *Liebestod,* the "model" marriage that confirms tortures finally felt in a real marriage, the degradation of her father (which doubles as the origin of guilt in the murder of the primal father) as a form of self-loathing, the loss of her father and husband like two suicides that leave the poet furiously fingering her scars—"Daddy" astonishes a reader by the subtle fury of its hurts.

The strong poetic personality that emerges in "Daddy" should remind a reader that the accomplishment of *Ariel* is first of all a stylistic one— what Ted Hughes calls its "crackling verbal energy." The exuberance is of a special sort. One would hesitate to term it "American," except that Plath herself did in a 1962 interview: "I think that as far as language goes I'm an American, I'm afraid, my accent is American, my way of talk is an American way of talk." The crucial dynamics, the sharp, quick tonal contrasts, the biting precision of word and image, the jaunty slang, the cinematic cutting, the high-power montage—these are what she is pointing to. Even in poems, like "Tulips," with quieter long lines, she sustains a new tension of menace and propulsion:

> My body is a pebble to them, they tend it as water
> Tends to the pebbles it must run over, smoothing them gently.
> They bring me numbness in their bright needles, they bring me
>   sleep.
> Now I have lost myself I am sick of baggage—
> My patent leather overnight case like a black pillbox,
> My husband and child smiling out of the family photo;
> Their smiles catch onto my skin, little smiling hooks.

In the book's best poems, the lines are pared down, at times to a stark, private code, but always with purity and exactness. Paradoxically, this taut, new control often creates effects of singular primitivism—the sense we have when encountering language used for rituals that precede literature, that impersonally participate in something more than they are. The seeming impersonality of the surfaces of the *Ariel* poems, as distinct from their private or confessional origin, derives from Plath's abundance and abandon, from the sense of autopsy she creates. There are several ways this has been achieved.

Though there are a few strong poems that employ two-line, pistonlike stanzas, her favorite stanza remained the tercet. The *Ariel* stanza must have developed from her earlier habit of terza rima, with its visual probity and stylized uniformity. But the freedom and variety of her new stanzas perfectly match the skittish, inflected voice that projects them. The lines in poems like "Lady Lazarus" and "Fever 103°" can be extended or retracted at will; often they prefer the shortness capable of sustaining a single word or phrase or fragment, giving it the prominence and strangeness of isolation. The thrusting surprise of line lengths is particularly apt for the continually shifting forms of address in, say, "Lady Lazarus," which jumps from invocation to question to command. It is steadied somewhat by the irregular use of rhyme, both internal and external, which establishes an aural "pattern" juxtaposed with the visual one. And Plath's canny use of repeated words and formulas has the same effect—appropriate to a poem that is less about suicide itself than about her obsessive, suicidal hatred of men and marriage, about loathing and self-hatred:

> So, so, Herr Doktor.
> So, Herr Enemy.
>
> I am your opus,
> I am your valuable,
> The pure gold baby
>
> That melts to a shriek.
> I turn and burn.
> Do not think I underestimate your great concern.
>
> Ash, ash—
> You poke and stir.
> Flesh, bone, there is nothing there—
>
> A cake of soap,
> A wedding ring,
> A gold filling.
>
> Herr God, Herr Lucifer,
> Beware
> Beware.
>
> Out of the ash
> I rise with my red hair
> And I eat men like air.

The aural sense of recurrence and the syntactic and visual irregularities together create an unsettling experience, one from which we have no time for distance as the poem, like many of Plath's late poems, rushes forward to exhaust itself. Where her early work was, in every sense, contained, *Ariel* operates at levels altogether more instinctual, uncertain, expelled. In these poems, there is less attention paid to explicit argument or rationale, to conceit or epiphany. To expropriate what her poem "Mystic" asks and answers, "Does the sea // Remember the walker upon it? / Meaning leaks from the molecules." Meaning, that is to say, derives not from the walker but from the water. The poet is not presider but medium, and the poem is not the expression of meaning but its conjuring context. And, for this effect, it is clearly her imagery Plath depended on in this book—the relentless succession of metaphors that seek out equivalence rather than comparison, identity rather than similarity. When such a technique seems unduly compulsive, as it does in "Cut," the result is dully self-indulgent. But a poem like "Edge" demonstrates brilliantly Plath's ability to induce a process—rather than construct a product—by the juxtaposition of paradoxical images rendered with the force of statement: the smiling corpse, the illusory necessity, the children as serpents (the Greek symbol of Necessity), the rose and the moon's night flower. During the course of this poem, the images meld with and become one another, a series of folding mirrors shifting in value and meaning—from the dead woman to the moon considered as female, an eerily animated dead stone dressed as the corpse is. And which is which?

These are the kinds of nondiscursive "deep images" that Robert Bly and James Wright were also exploring, though in *Ariel* Plath has done so with more conviction. Their programmatic "irrationalism" depends too heavily on accidental correspondences, avoiding as it does both metaphor and argument. Plath's approach was more enlightening, less erratic, and she was more successful than either Bly or Wright in getting beyond the mere physicality and discrete epiphanies of traditional imagism. Then too, poems like "Getting There," "Medusa," or "Little Fugue" make extensive use of the surrealism that poets like Robert Lowell would later turn to as, in Lowell's phrase, the "natural way to write our fictions," or the radical method of capturing the *natural* unreality of experience and of creating a new knowledge of it. Even the source of *Ariel*'s subject matter—no longer established themes in the suggested settings, but fragments of the occasional, accidental, domestic, or unconscious—has come to dominate much of the better work now being written. I am suggesting, in short, that Plath prefigured many of the decisive shifts in poetic strategy that occurred in the decade following her death. It is difficult to study her brief career for the kinds of substantial thematic complexities and continuities that one reads in Roethke or Lowell. But, considered from a stylistic viewpoint, Plath was as important an innovator as either of those poets. Her consistency and importance lie in her experiments with voice and the relationships among tone and image and address—axes after whose stroke the wood rings.

MARY LYNN BROE

The Bee Sequence:
"But I Have a Self to Recover"

In her six poems about the art of beekeeping, Plath attempts to "recover a self" by exploring the various operations of power within the apiary. The highly organized, self-regulating hive becomes her model for conceptualizing human experience by reexamining power in its many shapes (seller, keeper, worker drudge), or in its startling absence (queen). The poems suggest that there is a certain truth to psychologist David Holbrook's claim about Plath: "Be(e)ing seems a threat to one who doesn't know how to be."

We have observed Plath's imaginative investigations of inertia, her growing sensitivity to a belief in factual limitation. As early as her Cambridge Manuscript she realized that "though the mind like an oyster labors on and on, / a grain of sand is all we have." In *Crossing the Water* poems, the "Duchess of Nothing" announced boldly that "I housekeep in Time's gut-end / Among emmets and mollusks." Then she compared the task of mothering to the work of a cloud that distills a mirror in order to reflect its effacement by the wind. She attends to the moth-breath and horsehair simplicity of a small child. Too familiar with her own abstract truth and the "smashed blue hills" of her adult life, the mother "carpenters" a niche with her words for the child's "vowels like balloons." Her women personae are isolated, dismembered, even disappearing, but in each case, she resolves her investigation of passivity with a gesture of elusiveness that becomes her insurance against unwitting pain and vulnerability.

Now in the bee sequence Plath makes her most definitive and ambi-

From *Protean Poetic: The Poetry of Sylvia Plath.* © 1980 by the Curators of the University of Missouri. University of Missouri Press, 1980.

95

tious statement about passivity. She suggests that the absence of authoritative power is a form of strength and control, not merely a socially designated trait. Her focus includes only a few relationships and facts: the beekeeper's inept control over the apiary, the deceived workers and virgins, and the royal captive, that bare old queen in hiding whose productive reign over her hive has drawn to a close, but who still remains the focal point both in and outside the colony. While Plath explores the concept of power central to the hive community, her focus is on the ambivalence of the queen. Through this paradoxical symbol of power, she questions the implausible status of heroine in the special category of queen bee, and hence the complexities of a woman artist. For the queen's existence represents a kind of feminocide, a double-edged tribute to uniqueness best described by the workings of apiculture.

Beekeepers know that the queen's world is one moment of terribly limited splendor circumscribed by sacrifice: she has given up daylight, a voice in major hive decisions, such as swarming, freedom of flight, gathering the nectar of flowers, even some power in the matter of her own life or death—all for her worshiped prison of procreation. Her status is deceptive, for the real mind power and occupational unity of the hive reside in the liaison of thousands of short-lived workers who cower in their disguise of mediocrity. The queen, a symbol of ambiguous achievement, becomes the central means by which Plath examines the contradictory workings of power and the dimensions of the poetic self that might be recovered in the aesthetic process.

From the point of view of the speaker, the six bee poems describe a curve of maturation in their dramatic movement from youthful naiveté and disillusionment ("Beekeeper's Daughter") to vigorous exploration of contradictions inherent in power ("Arrival of the Bee Box," "The Bee Meeting," and "Stings"), and finally to a grasp of a new mode of power ("Wintering," "Swarm").

To begin to puzzle out the complex intermingling of life and death in the bee poems, we must first take Plath at her word:

> but I
> Have a self to recover, a queen.
> Is she dead, is she sleeping?
> Where has she been?

The narrative of the first poem in the series, "The Beekeeper's Daughter," is quite simple. The poet-child learns something about the pain and ecstasy of the "dark pa[i]rings" of sexuality within the bee kingdom. Her first glimpse of the apiarian world reveals the "maestro of bees" tending with ceremonial finesse the "many-breasted hives." She is fearful yet awed by the lush, androgynous sexuality in the miniature "garden of mouthings":

> The great corollas dilate, peeling back their silks.
>
> . . . .
>
> Trumpet-throats open to the beaks of birds.
> The Golden Rain Tree drips its powders down.

As she looks within the hive and contemplates with childish delight the queen bee's immortal reign over such uncontained fertility, she makes a rather stark discovery:

> The air is rich.
> Here is a queenship no mother can contest—
>
> A fruit that's death to taste: dark flesh, dark parings.
>
> . . . .
>
> I set my eye to a hole-mouth and meet an eye
> Round, green, disconsolate as a tear.

Looking for a reflection of herself—and the eye-I pun seems intentional—she finds only adult disillusionment and the unexpected complexity of a law that is central to the apiary. For the queen must suffer a uniquely regal motherhood. She neither directs nor participates in any of her subject's riches of cross-pollination. (The "uncontestable" queenship begins to sound slightly ironic.) For to one who never sees daylight, who has no bodily provisions for work, the virgin-workers' world of activity is really "death to taste." Literally, the fruit of flower (one meaning of "dark flesh, dark parings") is forbidden to this figurehead who remains ill-fated, hidden, and otherwise useless in her singular mission of motherhood.

Particularly significant about the queen's mission is its tragic nuptial flight, a blend of ecstasy and tragedy, life and death. It is in reference to this event that her first impressions are revised. She anticipates, first of all, the identification of father-maestro and the queen's mate, then the delusive power of sexual conquest and finally the union of death and sexuality in the remainder of the poem: "Father, bridegroom," she says, "the queen bee marries the winter of your year."

Apiarists know that the mate of the queen—chosen from thousands of suitors who pursue her high-spiraling nuptial flight—lives for a single moment of delight. But in this instant, the "dark pa[i]ring" is his undoing, the "winter of his year." For when he impregnates the queen, his abdomen splits open, loosing the entrails which the queen then totes behind her as a kind of triumphal banner. Dispensable, his death required for the propagation of the hive, the mate falls to the earth as a carcass; the queen, on the other hand, sports her murderous trophy, proof that she has guaranteed the future of the hive.

Within the poem, both maestro and bridegroom would seem to lose. The drone's taste of fruit in sexual union with the queen is costly. If we reexamine the poem with a purposeful child's-eye view, we see that the natural sexual world of the first half seems dark and funereal, forewarning the child's awakening. "Hieratical in his frock coat," the maestro suggests death as well as a wedding ceremony. Lush foliage smothers, asphyxiates, or is "nodding" or "dripping" as much with exhausted deadliness as with vitality:

> Purple, scarlet-speckled, black
> The great corollas dilate, peeling back their silks.
> Their musk encroaches, circle after circle
> A well of scents almost too dense to breath in.

As the child recognizes deathly, suffocating sexuality, her impression is echoed in the deadly nuptials of the queen bee and the father/bridegroom, the union of male and female principles. Neither the disconsolate queen nor her hapless male consort provides much encouragement to the young woman: the "wintry" drone dies, and the queen is but a tool of the hive's collective intent to ensure the future of the race. This is the rough adult lesson the maestro's daughter learns when her empathic "I" meets the "eye" of the old queen bee.

In sum, Plath's first bee poem anatomizes the process of discovery. The slow, calculated method by which the speaker arrives at awareness indirectly assumes importance over a smug, confident authority. The ambivalent imagery used to describe her growing awareness simulates a child's subliminal understanding that occurs gradually, well before the girl actually confronts the queen and grasps her paradoxical function.

The second poem in Plath's bee sequence, "The Bee Meeting," is a lengthy monologue that describes a mysterious rite of passage. The literal occasion, never made explicit, is a gathering of villagers who smoke out a beehive and get the honey. They move the virgin bees to another hive to prevent them from killing the old queen and, in this way, establish a new hive colony. A young girl is led by English country folk through various phases of an initiation ceremony where both the speaker's ignorance and the ambiguous imagery are calculated to suggest and sustain the life/death ambiguity of the event taking place.

But more important than either the literal occasion or our gradual discovery of it is the poem's focus on the speaker's emotional range and her implied identification with the queen, both central to the poem's meaning. Real power lies in the speaker's powerless ignorance about place, time, direction, and event, all the physical and metaphysical realities of the ceremony. ("Who are these people at the bridge to meet me? . . . why did nobody tell me?") Her disingenuousness ("I am nude as a chicken neck, does nobody love me?") and her fear of uniformity ("A black veil moulds to my face, they are making me one of them") prompt repeated questions that form the dramatic center of the poem. Since she feels fixed and controlled by the village professionals, her defense is to diminish herself in an act of mental powerlessness, willing her own inertia in the ambiguous event: "I cannot run, I am rooted, and the gorse hurts me. . . . If I stand very still, they will think I am cow parsley." Her choice for immobility is her only answer to those too-cheery voyeurs—the rector, sexton, and midwife—who merely witness the event, clapping one another in ritual gestures of approval.

Throughout the poem, the insistent questions of the naive young woman function in several ways. First, they signal that one is moving through and participating in an event. They shift the focus from the conclusion to the process of discovery. Finding the shape of the whole event undefined, the young woman feels increasing terror as the weight of every detail registers emotionally with her. "Is it some operation that is taking place," she asks, or are all these plateaus preparatory steps in bee etiquette? Is the progression—bridge to beanfield to the "shorn grove," the circle of hives, and finally to the empty chambers—a prescribed social ritual of conformity, or are we confronting the slow effacement of the dying process? Is this geography or mindscape?

The questions of the girl also sustain a powerful tension in imagery, keeping always before us the ambiguity between life and death, between scientific operation and transcendent ritual. Both the natural images (the beanfield and then the hawthorn grove) as well as the surgical imagery grow more ambiguous. They are comic yet deadly. Midwife, rector, and sexton are lumped together, "nodding square black heads." The rector, officiator at both deaths and entrances, chums with the midwife and the sexton during this formal ceremony, the three of them clad as sinister, depersonalized lookalikes. Vivid nature mingles with all that is antiseptically sterile:

> Strips of tinfoil winking like people,
> Feather dusters fanning their hands in a sea of bean flowers,
> Creamy bean flowers with black eyes and leaves like bored
>   hearts.

Gauzy white cheesecloth is set against black veils. The "milkweed silk" of a white garment hints at a hospital shift or a shroud slit ominously from neck to knee.

Even the technical details of beekeeping work paradoxically to sustain the life-death ambiguity. To avert death (the killing of the queen by her replacement), the virgins are moved by the villagers. To secure the future of the hive, a natural catastrophe ("smoking out") is simulated. Since smoke makes the bees emerge, believing their death to be imminent, it seems to the workers to be "the end of everything." Yet, for the queen, the smoking out is a new, if complex, freedom: "She is very clever. / She is old, old, old, she must live another year, and she knows it."

The traditional concept of power in the poem is paradoxical, relative, and, at best, suspect. The surgeon or mastermind of this mysterious operation is described as a science-fiction figure, a comic "apparition in a green helmet, / Shining gloves and white suit." Even the goodwilled villagers are wholly inept and clumsy. The speaker, ungloved and uncovered, is greeted by the high priests of conduct. Their garments scramble their identities and leave them looking like effete knights with no joust in sight: "Everybody is nodding a square black head, they are knights in visors, / Breastplates of cheesecloth knotted under the armpits." Physical power is undermined. Their confusing loss of identity is sad evidence of the need for collective disguise. Unanimous in their failure to make the most elementary distinctions between life and death, these folk conduct a witch-hunt through the hive's chambers and emerge with a misguided notion of their own success.

The controlling force of the poem is the shrewd queen bee, powerful in her very evasiveness. She proves her cleverness by refusing to show herself, whether to avoid a duel with the younger virgins or to escape some random fate from the villagers. To her, power is an attitude, a matter of perceiving life and death, the familiar and the terrible, simultaneously. She manipulates the visible from her vantage point of isolation. Physically, her fate is in others' hands. Mentally she remains untouched, undetected, her mind as well as her body "sealed in wax." Likewise, the inducted speaker—exhausted from the tedium of ignorance, fear, and unanswered questions—chooses immobility. Despite her outward conformity, she remains "a gullible head untouched by their [the bees'] animosity."

The poem's peculiar terror is that the link between the queen in her dotage and the young girl never becomes more overt than the final questions: "Whose is that long white box in the grove, what have they accomplished, why am I cold?" However, double-edged imagery and the speaker's helplessness intensify the identification. Both the queen and the speaker are mental rebels, yet physical pawns: the queen at the mercy of enterprising young virgins and villagers; the speaker besieged by workers on their "hysterical elastics," as well as by village elders. The queen eludes all forces of overt power. ("The old queen does not show herself, is she so ungrateful?") Likewise the speaker is physically passive, but conscious at every moment of the dramatic stakes of life and death:

> I am exhausted, I am exhausted—
> Pillar of white in a blackout of knives.
> I am the magician's girl who does not flinch.

In contrast to the naiveté of the first two poems, "Arrival of the Bee Box" is a prosaic study of rational control, of the brag of ownership, of the cheap physical coercion that can reject, kill, or merely unlock: "I ordered this, this clean wood box / Square as a chair and almost too heavy to lift." Assuming the power of the beekeeper-maestro, the speaker has ordered a box of undeveloped workers and finds herself faced with responsibility for their livelihood. "Tomorrow I will be sweet God, I will set them free," she asserts.

However, she deceives by her "unstable allegorical god-position" [as Barbara Hardy calls it], for the bulk of the poem reveals the obverse of the power that is authoritarian ownership. The bees control the speaker. As she becomes increasingly fascinated with their vitality and unintelligible noise, she abandons her declared pose of authority. She is lured to imagine various ways to dispose of the vital yet deadly threat:

> I have simply ordered a box of maniacs.
> They can be sent back.
> They can die, I need feed them nothing, I am the owner.

Again, a deathly vitality seems to overshadow any attempt to humorously diminish the contents of the dangerous bee box: the box is bursting with "maniacs," yet they are temporarily contained; they clamber vigorously with a "swarmy feeling," but still suggest decay ("African hands / Minute and shrunk for export"); reduced to a Roman mob chattering Latin, they are frighteningly alien. Whatever assertion of control has been cultivated in the tone, the imagery undercuts it. Her actual power becomes less convincing as her bravado grows. Fear, in fact, prompts her gradual stasis and effacement. She wildly scrambles the boundaries between herself and nature in a total defiance of the maestro's authority:

> I wonder if they would forget me
> If I just undid the locks and stood back and turned into a tree.

> There is the laburnum, its blond colonnades,
> And the petticoats of the cherry.

In the end, her grand resolve to play God is enfeebled by the boisterous liveliness of female drudges. Perhaps it is this sense of the bees' collective vitality that prompts the understated curious promise: "The box is only temporary."

After she recognizes the queen's isolation and the "dark pa[i]rings" of sexuality, a young girl dramatically experiences kinship with this paradoxical symbol of passivity. Miniature, invisible life ironically mocks the power of ownership. The speaker summarizes her progress in "Stings," a poem central to the developing drama of the bee sequence.

A scapegoat god whose presence was mere voyeurism has absconded from the poem. He is even less effective than the "maestro" father, the "imaginary god" who is owner of the bee box, or the life/death professionals who conduct the "Bee Meeting" ritual. Here the speaker successively dons the roles of beekeeper, honey-drudge, and queen in a dramatic exploration of their functions. "It is almost over / I am in control," she says midway through the process of adopting and then rejecting various selves. The comment is crucial and links the aesthetic and scientific levels of awareness in the poem and in the sequence: the speaker conducts us from the literal level of "sweet" bargaining for honey, through the equally mechanical collection of it by drudges, and, finally, to the queen's controlling *in*activity, her last triumph.

"Stings" opens with the speaker engaged in that simple bargaining procedure of exchanging honey for clean combs. But suddenly she finds brood cells "grey as the fossils of shells." This brief confrontation with silence prompts her poignant question about the metaphysics of be(e)ing: "Is there any queen at all in it?" After this question, she shifts quickly to the imagined role of worker standing in a "column of unmiraculous women." Their "scurry," their cheerful mechanical existence, ignores a life of the mind. The speaker's link to these "industrious virgins" is her own honey-machine, the extractor:

> It will work without thinking,
>
> . . . .
>
> To scour creaming crests
> As the moon, for its ivory powders, scours the sea.

Unlike gathering honey from the "open cherry, the open clover," extracting honey from the cells is an arid, derivative process. The speaker's "strangeness" may be tenuous and likely to evaporate ("blue dew from dangerous skin"), but she is no drudge. Worker-drudges are easily deceived in their unconscious activity of searching for honey. Only too late do they discover their own deception, as happened with the poem's interloper:

> The bees found him out,
> Moulding onto his lips like lies,
> Complicating his features.

Although the bees obscure his identity with their stings, the cost to these workers is life itself, since honeybees die after they sting.

The speaker realizes—from the misleading third person now fled and from the impressionable workers—that no one, nothing, is worth sacrificing one's life for:

> They thought death was worth it, but I
> Have a self to recover, a queen.
> Is she dead, is she sleeping?
> Where has she been,
> With her lion-red body, her wings of glass?

The final image of the resurrected (recovered) queen is central to the bee sequence. The longtime elusive self, now visible, is a surprising triumph of contradictions. While most critics do recognize the importance of Plath's kinship with this bare, "plushless" queen, they nevertheless claim that it is "evidently only in death, if ever, that the queen, the persona (the identification seems complete), will recover her unique self"(Ingrid Melander, *The Poetry of Sylvia Plath: A Study of Themes*).

But it is not death that is the "liberator of her unique personality." It is a peculiar meshing of those vital contradictions and the ritual, imagined deaths. Such contradictions have been at the very center of the life-death imagery throughout the sequence and culminate here in this recovery. Is hers a transcendence? A rebirth to death? A political exorcising of husband/father/domesticity, or [as Judith Kroll puts it] a triumph over the male "to whom the false self has been servile?" The movement through various roles central to the sequence, now enacted within the microcosm "Stings," has prepared the way for this self-styled queen of contradictions. The authoritative mode, seen in simple bartering and in the voyeur-god of "Stings," has been abandoned.

Like many of Plath's later high-energy poems ("Lady Lazarus," "Fever 103°"), "Stings" presents an ambivalence that makes the recovered queen image more realistic, more credible. The queen's feminocide is implicit in her action as well as in the persistent dualistic imagery. Queenship is a double-bind situation where the special category carries with it the threat of fossilization. The hive killed the queen by entombing her powers in its sealed waxen brood cells. She became a narrowly defined reproductive symbol and suffered a kind of death-in-life, the feminocidal hazard of "specialness." Now, however, the queen is:

> flying
> More terrible than she ever was, red
> Scar in the sky, red comet
> Over the engine that killed her—
> The mausoleum, the wax house.

She is, to be sure, no antique replica emerging from "wormy mahogany." Imagery of transcendence commingles with hints of illness, vulnerability ("red scar," "her wings of glass") with ferocity ("lion-red body," "red comet"), to fashion a surprisingly resilient and vital queen. She both conquers and recognizes limitations.

After the queen's triumphal flight over "the mausoleum" in "Stings," "Wintering" praises the workers for their minimal survival. "It is they who own me," the keeper says of these workers who barely hang on, so slow that they are hardly recognizable. They possess the beekeeper by their sheer power of knowing how to survive ("neither cruel nor indifferent, / Only ignorant"), and how to scale subsistence down according to hibernal limitations. They endure the natural elements, the habits of the sponging drones, and even turn the deceptions of traditional authority (Tate and Lyle artificial sugar for honey) into life sustenance. The sugar ("refined snow") hints of the commingling of life and death: what nourishes the bees through the long winter appears to be like the white snow in which they bury their dead.

A deceptively profound efficiency governs this dark hibernaculum "at the heart of the house." The perfunctory labor of extracting honey has not prepared the beekeeper for the activities within the smothering room. After her initial boast ("This is the easy time, there is nothing doing. / I have whirled the midwife's extractor, / I have my honey"), the speaker faces a growing horror that her power is neither deep nor comprehensive enough to grasp so much sweetness with so much deathly decay. The beekeeper is no more a match for this inertia than she was for the puzzling, boxed vitality in "Arrival of the Bee Box":

> This is the room I have never been in.
> This is the room I could never breathe in.

The black bunched in there like a bat,
No light
But the torch and its faint

Chinese yellow on appalling objects—
Black asininity. Decay.
Possession.

Fearless, "rid of the men" now ("the blunt, clumsy stumblers, the boors"), these bees, all of whom are women, make a life for themselves "wintering in the dark without a window / At the heart of the house." Why? Because unlike the smug keeper whose efficiency is outwardly directed, these bees are self-determining. Their ability to perceive, accept, and project the reality of inner states is surely as purposeful as that "woman, still at her knitting, / At the cradle of Spanish walnut, / Her body a bulb in the cold and too dumb to think." Implicit in the poem's final seasonal renewal is criticism of the beekeeper's defunct power that misunderstands inwardness. The beekeeper is possessed by neither cruelty nor indifference, but by those who collectively outlast death, fraudulence, cold, and grand expectations. These workers, in the end, "are flying." It is they who "taste the spring."

From praise for minimal activity in "Wintering," Plath moves to consider the historical plight of imaginative versus physical power in "The Swarm." "How instructive this is," she sarcastically remarks as she watches the antics of the man with a gun who attempts to shoot down a swarming hive. Two kinds of power—physical, self-defensive will (the smiling practical man with "grey hands"), and visionary, collective dreams (the "black intractable" mind of the swarm)—cancel each other out within the poem. By mutual deception and delusion, both are reduced to "the white busts of marshals, admirals, generals / Worming themselves into niches" like white grubs germinating in hive cells.

It would appear that because the practical man with the gun and "asbestos receptacles" for hands can topple dreams to mere facts, or shoot fantasy hives into "cocked straw hats" ("Seventy feet high! / Russia, Poland and Germany . . . fields shrunk to a penny"), his power is triumphant: "Pom! Pom! They fall / Dismembered to a tod of ivy." Although he may have physical force and protective garb, his greed for honey, his contempt for bees, and his fear of stings ("It is you the knives are out for") prompt a feeble self-defense: "They would have killed *me*." In his misunderstanding of the bees' natural swarming patterns, he knows that "seventy feet up" is out of his control, and that he must exert corrective force:

> The dumb, banded bodies
> Walking the plank draped with Mother France's upholstery
> Into a new mausoleum,
> An ivory palace, a crotch pine.

The swarm is also deceived in several ways. Deserting to their "black pine tree," they mistake a gun for thunder ("the voice of God / Condoning the beak, the claw, the grin of the dog"). They are victims of self-delusion. The collective mind is prey to the aspirations of a Napoleon with his master plan for the "charioteers, the outriders, the Grand Army": "their dream, the hived station / Where trains, faithful to their steel arcs, / Leave and arrive, and there is no end to the country." Their absolute "notion of honor" causes them to sting the man with the gun who is a threat to their plans. Such action not only costs the bees their lives but exaggerates their failure to accept real limitations (the "tod of ivy," the "cocked straw hat," "stings big as drawing pins").

Central to the poem is the context of Napoleonic history that diminishes both the gunman's individual will-to-power and the swarm's collective delusions of grandeur. The bee itself, a public symbol of order in the sixteenth century and a private emblem for Napoleon, is ridiculed by this imagery. Either sort of power here is derivative; either is dependent upon some other person or force for definition. Of the so-called instructive aspects of the poem, it has been said [by David Holbrook] that "from her own deep need to feel real, to be human, Plath can see the Napoleonic impulse to be Great through Hate with irony." A psychic distance is gained by these cultural references. They puncture victories, dreams, jealousies that can "open the blood," greed, strengths, and even exiles, making them no more than a network of collective deceptions. Surely there is something mock-epic about Napoleon's conquests being reduced to arguing bees, "a flying hedgehog, all prickles," or to a "man with asbestos gloves" training his gun on bees in a tree. "Elba, Elba, bleb on the sea," the speaker chants in anagrammatic playfulness, pointing up the defeat of all grand aims "knocked into a cocked straw hat" of a hive. This mockery includes the practical gunman who believes he is more authentic than the bees:

> Shh! These are chess people you play with,
> Still figures of ivory.
> The mud squirms with throats,
> Stepping stones for French bootsoles.
> The gilt and pink domes of Russia melt and float off
>
> In the furnace of greed. Clouds, clouds.

Throughout her poetic investigation, Plath has formulated a new valuation for passivity based on the function of power within the hierarchy of the apiary, and most particularly on the interrelationship of the old queen, the beekeeper, and the workers, who are specialists in minimal survival. Plath has discovered that the power of inertia is, paradoxically, one of the greatest literary possibilities for contemporary women. Such "abandonment of authority as a rhetorical pose," is a point clarified by Patricia Spacks and Mary Ellmann [in Spacks's *The Female Imagination*]:

> In our time, the "authoritative mode is no longer the mode of original, which is more than competent expression. At the same time, the exertion of sensibility is not marked in the most interesting writing by women now." The temper of the age is such that claims of authority are now likely to seem ludicrous.

Passivity reevaluated as a form of power in the bee sequence is markedly different from the "Great Multiple Lie [about female nature] freshly got up in drag" that is described by Cynthia Ozick [in "Does Genius Have a Gender?" *Ms.*]. According to Ozick, the new feminist strategy of isolating a female nature—a kind of "voluntary circumscription"—is really aimed toward the same authoritarian end as the old hostile, biologically based self-confinement:

> Thurber once wrote a story about a bear who leaned so far backward that he ended up by falling on his face. Now we are enduring a feminism so far advanced into "new truths" that it has arrived at last at a set of notions undistinguishable from the most age-encrusted, unenlightened, and imprisoning antifeminist views.

Again we see Plath rejecting the socially determined "new truth" of passivity (with its corollaries of evasiveness, indirection, deviousness, and apology) as a weakness. Instead, she assigns to passivity a positive value of choice, not of social situation, a function that Plath has already imaginatively dramatized in earlier poetry. The worst deception to Plath—seen repeatedly in her female images and culminating in the queen bee—is the act of merely subscribing to one's nature, unexamined. Rather, Plath is always in control of the kaleidoscopic selves that she explores in the process of trying to understand the limits of traditional power and the function of passivity. For her, passivity becomes an investigative resource, never so thoroughly yet succinctly stated as in her bee sequence.

"I have a self to recover," she asserts as she carves out a new value for contradiction. From a child's recognition of the paradoxical isolation and "dark pa[i]rings" of the queen bee, Plath's young speaker dramatically identifies with her in "Bee Meeting." The sheer vitality of those hidden but controlling female forces in "Arrival of the Bee Box" overpowers physical authority while the image of the angry red queen represents a new tolerance for contradictions in "Stings." In "Wintering," physical authority is possessed by the apparently passive and resigned worker bees and queen. Finally, in "Swarm," both physical and imaginative control are canceled out by Plath's mockery.

The commingling of life and death has strengthened the power of inertia in its many examples within the sequence: the "disconsolate" queen in her burrow; the double-edged survival of the workers in winter; the ambivalence of the red queen in "Stings." The many shifts in tone—naive wonderment, simple declaration, mock-epic allusiveness—show Plath exploring aesthetic possibilities as well as enlarging her tonal authority.

Her exploration within the apiary has developed originally, dramatically, in a crescendo that describes the "process of constructing meaning" [to quote Dorin Schumacher's phrase in *Feminist Literary Criticism: Explorations in Theory,* ed. Josephine Donovan], not the correctness of a fixed body of critical facts about apiculture, power, or the "new feminism." Within the microcosm of the bee world and this six-poem sequence, Plath's new space carved for contradictions suggests, once again, the rival energies at work in the late poems: the triumphal energy of performance coexists with a small constructiveness and counseled limitations. The late poems pose a challenge to the poet. As she realizes the benefits of being small, inert, and leading the scaled-down life, she also realizes that she is condemned to a state of complexity and continual change. Despite her knowledge that she had indeed "one too many dimensions to enter," Plath is still drawn to the difficult enlarged vision where neutrality and physical simplicity coexist with "some things of this world that are indigestible."

TED HUGHES

Sylvia Plath and Her Journals

Sylvia Plath's journals exist as an assortment of notebooks and bunches of loose sheets, and the selection just published contains about a third of the whole bulk. Two other notebooks survived for a while after her death. They continued from where the surviving record breaks off in late 1959 and covered the last three years of her life. The second of these two books her husband destroyed, because he did not want her children to have to read it (in those days he regarded forgetfulness as an essential part of survival). The earlier one disappeared more recently (and may, presumably, still turn up).

The motive in publishing these journals will be questioned. The argument against is still strong. A decisive factor has been certain evident confusions, provoked in the minds of many of her readers by her later poetry. *Ariel* is dramatic speech of a kind. But to what persona and to what drama is it to be fitted? The poems don't seem to supply enough evidence of the definitive sort. This might have been no bad thing, if a riddle fertile in hypotheses is a good one. But the circumstances of her death, it seems, multiplied every one of her statements by a wild, unknown quantity. The results, among her interpreters, have hardly been steadied by the account she gave of herself in her letters to her mother, or by the errant versions supplied by her biographers. So the question grows: how do we find our way through this accompaniment, which has now become almost a part of the opus? Would we be helped if we had more firsthand testimony, a more intimately assured image, of what she was really like? In answer to this, these papers, which contain the nearest thing to a living portrait of her, are offered in the hope of providing

From *Grand Street* 1, no. 3 (Spring 1982). © 1982 by Ted Hughes and Grand Street Publications, Inc.

some ballast for our idea of the reality behind the poems. Maybe they will do more.

Looking over this curtailed journal, we cannot help wondering whether the lost entries for her last three years were not the more important section of it. Those years, after all, produced the work that made her name. And we certainly have lost a valuable appendix to all that later writing. Yet these surviving diaries contain something that cannot be less valuable. If we read them with understanding, they can give us the key to the most intriguing mystery about her, the key to our biggest difficulty in our approach to her poetry.

That difficulty is the extreme peculiarity in kind of her poetic gift. And the difficulty is not lessened by the fact that she left behind two completely different kinds of poetry.

Few poets have disclosed in any way the birth circumstances of their poetic gift, or the necessary purpose these serve in their psychic economy. It is not easy to name one. As if the first concern of poetry were to cover its own tracks. When a deliberate attempt to reveal all has been made, by a Pasternak or a Wordsworth, the result is discursive autobiography—illuminating enough, but not an X-ray. Otherwise poets are very properly bent on exploring subject matter, themes, intellectual possibilities and modifications, evolving the foliage and blossoms and fruit of a natural cultural organism whose roots are hidden, and whose birth and private purpose are no part of the crop. Sylvia Plath's poetry, like a species on its own, exists in little else but the revelation of that birth and purpose. Though her whole considerable ambition was fixed on becoming the normal flowering and fruiting kind of writer, her work was roots only. Almost as if her entire oeuvre were enclosed within those processes and transformations that happen in other poets before they can even begin, before the muse can hold out a leaf. Or as if all poetry were made up of the feats and shows performed by the poetic spirit Ariel. Whereas her poetry is the biology of Ariel, the ontology of Ariel—the story of Ariel's imprisonment in the pine, before Prospero opened it. And it continued to be so even after the end of *The Colossus*, which fell, as it happens, in the last entries of this surviving bulk of her journal, where the opening of the pine took place and was recorded.

This singularity of hers is a mystery—an enigma in itself. It may be that she was simply an extreme case, that many other poets' works nurse and analyze their roots as doggedly as hers do, but that she is distinguished by an unusually clear root system and an abnormally clear and clinically exact system of attending to it. It may be something to do with the fact that she was a woman. Maybe her singularity derives from a feminine beeline instinct for the real priority, for what truly matters—an instinct for nursing and repairing the damaged and threatened nucleus of the self and for starving every other aspect of her life in order to feed and strengthen that, and bring that to a safe delivery.

The root system of her talent was a deep and inclusive inner crisis which seems to have been quite distinctly formulated in its chief symbols (presumably going back at least as far as the death of her father, when she was ten) by the time of her first attempted suicide, in 1953, when she was twenty-one.

After 1953, it became a much more serious business, a continuous hermetically sealed process that changed only very slowly, so that for years it looked like deadlock. Though its preoccupation dominated her life, it remained largely outside her ordinary consciousness, but in her poems we see the inner working of it. It seems to have been scarcely disturbed at all by the outer upheavals she passed through, by her energetic involvement in her studies, in her love affairs and her marriage, and in her jobs, though she used details from them as a matter of course for images to develop her X-rays.

The importance of these diaries lies in the rich account they give of her attempts to understand this obscure process, to follow it, and (in vain) to hasten it. As time went on, she interpreted what was happening to her inwardly, more and more consciously, as a "drama" of some sort. After its introductory overture (everything up to 1953), the drama proper began with a "death," which was followed by a long "gestation" or "regeneration," which in turn would ultimately require a "birth" or a "rebirth," as in Dostoevsky and Lawrence and those other prophets of rebirth whose works were her sacred books.

The "death," so important in all that she wrote after it, was that almost successful suicide attempt in the summer of 1953. The mythical dimensions of the experience seem to have been deepened, and made absolute, and illuminated, by two accidents: she lay undiscovered, in darkness, only intermittently half-conscious, for "three days"; and the electric shock treatment which followed went wrong, and she was all but electrocuted—at least so she always claimed. Whether it did and she was, or not, there seems little doubt that her "three day" death, and that thunderbolt awakening, fused her dangerous inheritance into a matrix from which everything later seemed to develop—as from a radical change in the structure of her brain.

She would describe her suicide attempt as a bid to get back to her father, and one can imagine that in her case this was a routine reconstruction, from a psychoanalytical point of view. But she made much of it, and it played an increasingly dominant role in her recovery and in what her poetry was able to become. Some of the implications might be divined from her occasional dealings with the Ouija board, during the late fifties. Her father's name was Otto, and "spirits" would regularly arrive with instructions for her from one Prince Otto, who was said to be a great power in the underworld. When she pressed for a more personal communication, she would be told that Prince Otto could not speak to her directly, because he was under orders from The Colossus. And when she pressed for an audience with The Colossus, they would say he was inaccessible. It is easy to see how her effort to come to terms with the meaning this Colossus held for her, in her poetry, became more and more central as the years passed.

The strange limbo of "gestation/regeneration," which followed her "death," lasted throughout the period of this journal, and she drew from the latter part of it all the poems of *The Colossus,* her first collection. We have spoken of this process as a "nursing" of the "nucleus of the self," as a hermetically sealed, slow transformation of her inner crisis; and the evidence surely supports these descriptions of it as a deeply secluded mythic and symbolic inner theater (sometimes a hospital theater), accessible to her only in her poetry. One would like to emphasize even more strongly the weird autonomy of what was going on in there. It gave the impression of being a secret crucible, or rather a womb, an almost biological process—and just as much beyond her manipulative interference. And like a pregnancy, selfish with her resources.

We can hardly make too much of this special condition, both in our understanding of her journal and in our reading of the poems of her first book. A reader of the journal might wonder why she did not make more of day-to-day events. She had several outlandish adventures during these years, and interesting things were always happening to her. But her diary entries habitually ignore them. When she came to talk to herself in these pages, that magnetic inner process seemed to engross all her attention, one way or another. And in her poems and stories, throughout this period, she felt her creative dependence on that same process as subjection to a tyrant. It commandeered every proposal. Many passages in [the journals] show the deliberate—almost frantic—effort with which she tried to extend her writing, to turn it toward the world and other people, to stretch it over more of outer reality, to forget herself in some exploration of outer reality—in which she took, after all, such constant, intense delight. But the hidden workshop, the tangle of roots, the crucible, controlled everything. Everything became another image of itself, another lens into itself. And whatever it could not use in this way, to objectify some disclosure of itself, did not get onto the page at all.

Unless we take account of this we shall almost certainly misread the moods of her journal—her nightmare sense of claustrophobia and suspended life, her sense of being only the flimsy, brittle husk of what was going heavily and fierily on, somewhere out of reach inside her. And we shall probably find ourselves looking into her poems for things and qualities which could only be there if that process had been less fiercely concentrated on its own purposeful chemistry. We shall misconstrue the tone and content of the poetry that did manage to transmit from the center, and the psychological exactness and immediacy of its mournful, stressful confinement.

A Jungian might call the whole phase a classic case of the alchemical individuation of the self. This interpretation would not tie up every loose end, but it would make positive meaning of the details of the poetic imagery— those silent horrors going on inside a glass crucible, a crucible that reappears in many forms, but always glassy and always closed. Above all, perhaps, it would help to confirm a truth—that the process was, in fact, a natural and positive process, if not the most positive and healing of all involuntary responses to the damage of life: a process of self-salvation—a resurrection of her deepest spiritual vitality against the odds of her fate. And the Jungian interpretation would fit the extraordinary outcome too: the birth of her new creative self.

The significant thing, even so, in the progress she made, was surely the way she applied herself to the task. Her battered and so-often-exhausted determination, the relentless way she renewed the assault without ever really knowing what she was up against. The seriousness, finally, of her will to face what was wrong in herself, and to drag it out into examination, and to remake it—that is what is so impressive. Her refusal to rest in any halfway consolation or evasive delusion. And it produced some exemplary pieces of writing, here and there, in her diaries. It would not be so impressive if she were not so manifestly terrified of doing what she nevertheless did. At times, she seems almost invalid in her lack of inner protections. Her writing here (as in her poems) simplifies itself in baring itself to what hurts her. It is unusually devoid of intellectual superstructures—of provisional ideas, theorizings, developed fantasies, which are all protective clothing as well as tools. What she did have, clearly, was character—and passionate character at that. One sees where the language of *Ariel* got its temper—that unique blend of courage and vulnerability. The notion of her forcing herself, in her "Japanese silks, desperate butterflies," deeper into some internal furnace, strengthens throughout these pages, and remains.

But she was getting somewhere. Late in 1959 (toward the end of the surviving diaries) she had a dream, which at the time made a visionary impact on her, in which she was trying to reassemble a giant, shattered, stone Colossus. In the light of her private mythology, we can see this dream was momentous, and she versified it, addressing the ruins as "Father," in a poem which she regarded, at the time, as a breakthrough. But the real significance of the dream emerges, perhaps, a few days later, when the quarry of anthropomorphic ruins reappears, in a poem titled "The Stones." In this second poem, the ruins are no other than the hospital city, the factory where men are remade, and where, among the fragments, a new self has been put together. Or rather an old shattered self, reduced by violence to its essential core, has been repaired and renovated and born again, and—most significant of all—speaks with a new voice.

This "birth" is the culmination of her prolonged six-year "drama." It is doubtful whether we would be reading this journal at all if the "birth" recorded in that poem, "The Stones," had not happened in a very real sense, in November 1959.

The poem is the last of a sequence titled "Poem for a Birthday." Her diary is quite informative about her plans for this piece, which began as little more than an experimental poetic idea that offered scope for her to play at imitating Roethke. But evidently there were hidden prompters. As a piece of practical magic, "Poem for a Birthday" came just at the right moment. Afterward, she knew something had happened, but it is only in retrospect that we can see what it was. During the next three years she herself came to view this time as the turning point in her writing career, the point where her real writing began.

Looking back further, maybe we can see signs and portents before then. Maybe her story "Johnny Panic and the Bible of Dreams" was the John the Baptist. And in her own recognition of the change, at the time, she spread the honors over several other poems as well—"The Manor Garden" (which is an apprehensive welcome to the approaching unborn), "The Colossus" (which is the poem describing the visionary dream of the ruined Colossus), and "Medallion" (which describes a snake as an undead, unliving elemental beauty, a crystalline essence of stone). But this poem, "The Stones," is the thing itself.

It is unlike anything that had gone before in her work. The system of association, from image to image and within the images, is quite new, and—as we can now see—it is that of *Ariel*. And throughout the poem what we hear coming clear is the now-familiar voice of *Ariel*.

In its double focus, "The Stones" is both a "birth" and a "rebirth." It is the birth of her real poetic voice, but it is the rebirth of herself. That poem encapsulates, with literal details, her "death," her treatment, and her slow, buried recovery. And this is where we can see the peculiarity of her imagination at work, where we can see how the substance of her poetry and the very substance of her survival are the same. In another poet, "The Stones" might have been an artistic assemblage of fantasy images. But she was incapable of free fantasy, in the ordinary sense. If an image of hers had its source in sleeping or waking "dream," it was inevitably the image of some meaning she had paid for or would have to pay for, in some way— that she had lived or would have to live. It had the *necessity* of a physical symptom. This is the objectivity of her subjective mode. Her internal crystal ball was helplessly truthful, in this sense. (And truthfulness of that sort has inescapable inner consequences.) It determined her lack of freedom, sure enough, as we have already seen. But it secured her loyalty to what was, for her, the most important duty of all. And for this reason the succession of images in "The Stones," in which we see her raising a new self out of the ruins of her mythical father, has to be given the status of fact. The "drama," in which she redeemed and balanced the earlier "death" with this "birth/rebirth," and from which she drew so much confidence later on, was a great simplification, but we cannot easily doubt that it epitomizes, in ritual form, the main inner labor of her life up to the age of twenty-seven.

And this is the story her diaries have to tell: how a poetic talent was forced into full expressive being, by internal need, for a purpose vital to the whole organism.

"Birth," of the sort we have been talking about, is usually found in the context of a religion, or at least of some mystical discipline. It is rare in secular literature. If "The Stones" does indeed record such a birth, we should now look for some notable effects, some exceptional flowering of energy. It is just this second phase of her career that has proved so difficult to judge in conventional literary terms. But whatever followed November 1959, in Sylvia Plath's writing, has a bearing on our assessment of what is happening in this journal.

Shortly after the date of the last poems of *The Colossus,* and the last date of her diary proper, a big change did come over her life. It took a few weeks to get into its stride.

When she sailed for England in December with her husband, though she had her new, full-formed confidence about her writing to cheer her, her life still seemed suspended, and all her ambitions as far off as ever. In a poem she wrote soon after, "On Deck," she mentions that one of her fellow passengers on the *S.S. United States,* an American astrologer—he was physically a double for James Joyce—had picked that most propitious date for launching his astrological conquest of the British public. His optimism did not rub off on her. With her last college days well behind her, and only writing and maternity ahead, the December London of 1959 gave her a bad shock—the cars seemed smaller and blacker and dingier than ever, sizzling through black wet streets. The clothes on the people seemed even grubbier than she remembered. And when she lay on a bed in a basement room in a scruffy hotel near Victoria, a week or two later with *The Rack,* by A. E. Ellis, propped open on her pregnant stomach, it seemed to her she had touched a new nadir.

Yet within the next three years she achieved one after another almost all the ambitions she had been brooding over in frustration for the last decade. In that first month her collection of poems *The Colossus* was taken for publication in England by Heinemann. With that out of the way, in April she produced a daughter. In early 1961, at high speed, and in great exhilaration, she wrote her autobiographical novel *The Bell Jar,* and though both Harper and Knopf rejected it in the States, Heinemann took it at once for publication in England. One important part of her life-plan was to acquire a "base," as she called it, somewhere in England, from which she hoped to make her raids on the four corners of the earth, devouring the delights and excitements. And accordingly, later in 1961, she acquired a house in the West of England. In January of 1962 she produced a son. In May of that year *The Colossus* was published in the States by Knopf.

Meanwhile, she went on steadily writing her new poems. After the promise of "The Stones," we look at these with fresh attention. And they *are* different from what had gone before. But superficially not very different. For one thing, there is little sign of *Ariel.* And she herself seemed to feel that these pieces were an interlude. She published them in magazines, but otherwise let them lie—not exactly rejected by her, but certainly not coaxed anxiously toward a next collection, as this journal shows her worrying over her earlier poems. The demands of her baby occupied her time, but this does not entirely explain the lull in her poetry. The poems themselves, as before, reveal what was going on.

Everything about her writing at this time suggests that after 1959, after she had brought her "death-rebirth" drama to a successful issue, she found herself confronted, on that inner stage, by a whole new dramatic situation— one that made her first drama seem no more than the preliminaries, before the lifting of the curtain.

And in fact that birth, which had seemed so complete in "The Stones," was dragging on. And it went on dragging on. We can follow the problem- atic accouchement in the poems. They swing from the apprehensions of a woman or women of sterility and death at one extreme, to joyful maternal celebration of the living and almost-born fetus at the other—with one or two encouraging pronouncements from the oracular fetus itself in between.

But evidently much had still to be done. Perhaps something like the writing of *The Bell Jar* had still to be faced and got through. It is not until we come to the poems of September, October, and November of 1961—a full two years after "The Stones"—that the newborn seems to feel the draft of the outer world. And even now the voice of *Ariel,* still swaddled in the old mannerisms, is hardly more than a whimper. But at least we can see what the new situation is. We see her new self confronting—to begin with—the sea, not just the sea off Finisterre and off Hartland, but the Bay of the Dead, and "nothing, nothing but a great space"—which becomes the surgeon's 2 A.M. ward of mutilations (reminiscent of the hospital city in "The Stones"). She confronts her own moon-faced sarcophagus, her mirror clouding over, the moon in its most sinister aspect, and the yews—"blackness and silence." In this group of poems—the most chilling pieces she had written up to this time—what she confronts is all that she had freed herself from.

Throughout the *Colossus* poems, as we have seen, the fateful part of her being, the part—a large, inclusive complex—that had formerly been too much for her, had held her, as a matrix, and nursed her back to new life. Death, in this matrix (and in one sense the whole complex, which had tried to kill her and had all but succeeded, came under the sign of death), had a homeopathic effect on the nucleus that survived.

But now that she was resurrected, as a self that she could think of as an Eve (as she tried so hard to do in her radio play "Three Women"), a lover of life and of her children, she still had to deal with everything in her that remained otherwise, everything that had held her in the grave for "three days," The Other. And, it was only now, for the first time, at her first step into independent life, that she could see it clearly for what it was—confronting her, separated from her at last, to be contemplated and, if possible, overcome.

It is not hard to understand her despondency at this juncture. Her new Ariel self had evolved for the very purpose of winning this battle, and much as she would have preferred, most likely, to back off and live in some sort of truce, her next step was just as surely inescapable.

From her new position of strength, she came to grips quite quickly. After *Three Women* (which has to be heard, as naïve speech, rather than read as a literary artifact) quite suddenly the ghost of her father reappears, for the first time in two and a half years, and meets a daunting, point-blank, demythologized assessment. This is followed by the most precise description she ever gave of The Other—the deathly woman at the heart of everything she now closed in on. After this, her poems arrived at a marvelous brief poise. Three of them together, titled "Crossing the Water," "Among the Narcissi"

and "Pheasant," all written within three or four days of one another in early
April 1962, are unique in her work. And maybe it was this achievement,
inwardly, this cool, light, very beautiful moment of mastery, that enabled her
to take the next step.

Within a day or two of writing "Pheasant," she started a poem about a
giant wych elm that overshadowed the yard of her home. The manuscript of
this piece reveals how she began it in her usual fashion, as another poem of
the interlude, maybe a successor to "Pheasant" (the actual pheasant of the
poem had flown up into the actual elm) and the customary features began to
assemble. But then we see a struggle break out, which continues over several
pages, as the lines try to take the law into their own hands. She forced the
poem back into order, and even got a stranglehold on it, and seemed to have
won, when suddenly it burst all her restraints and she let it go.

And at once the *Ariel* voice emerged in full. From that day on, it never
really faltered again. During the next five months she produced ten more
poems. The subject matter didn't alarm her. Why should it, when Ariel
was doing the very thing it had been created and liberated to do? In each
poem, the terror is encountered head on, and the angel is mastered and
brought to terms. The energy released by these victories was noticeable.
According to the appointed coincidence of such things, after July her outer
circumstances intensified her inner battle to the limits. In October, when she
and her husband began to live apart, every detail of the antagonist seemed
to come into focus, and she started writing at top speed, producing twenty-
six quite lengthy poems in that month. In November she produced twelve,
with another on December 1st and one more on December 2nd before the
flow stopped abruptly.

She now began to look for a flat in London. In December she found
a maisonette, in a house adorned with a plaque commemorating the fact
that Yeats had lived there, near Primrose Hill. She decorated this place,
furnished it prettily, moved in with her children before Christmas, and set
about establishing a circle of friends.

By this time she knew quite well what she had brought off in October and November. She knew she had written beyond her wildest dreams.
And she had overcome, by a stunning display of power, the bogies of her
life. Yet her attitude to the poems was detached. "They saved me," she
said, and spoke of them as an episode that was past. And indeed it was
blazingly clear that she had come through, in Lawrence's sense, and that
she was triumphant. The impression of growth and new large strength in
her personality was striking. The book lay completed, the poems carefully
ordered. And she seemed to be under no compulsion to start writing again.

On December 31st she tinkered with a poem that she had drafted in October but had not included in the *Ariel* canon, and even now she did not bother to finish it—one of the few poems (only two or three in her mature career) that she did not carry through to a finished copy.

In January of 1963 what was called the coldest freeze-up in fifteen years affected her health and took toll of her energy. She was in resilient form, however, for the English publication of *The Bell Jar* on January 23rd. If she felt any qualms at the public release of this supercharged piece of her autobiography, she made no mention of it at the time, either in conversation or in her diary. Reading them now, the reviews seem benign enough, but at the time, like all reviews, they brought exasperation and dismay. But they did not visibly deflate her.

Then on January 28th she began to write again. She considered these poems a fresh start. She liked the different, cooler inspiration (as she described it) and the denser pattern, of the first of these, as they took shape. With after-knowledge, one certainly looks at something else—though the premonitory note, except maybe in her very last poem, is hardly more insistent than it had seemed in many an earlier piece.

But in that first week of February a number—a perverse number—of varied crises coincided. Some of these have been recounted elsewhere. No doubt all of them combined to give that unknowable element its chance, in her final act, on the early morning of Monday, February 11th.

All her poems are in a sense by-products. Her real creation was that inner gestation and eventual birth of a new self-conquering self, to which her journal bears witness, and which proved itself so overwhelmingly in the *Ariel* poems of 1962. If this is the most important task a human being can undertake (and it must surely be one of the most difficult), then this is the importance of her poems, that they provide such an intimate, accurate embodiment of the whole process from beginning to end—or almost to the end.

That her new self, who could do so much, could not ultimately save her, is perhaps only to say what has often been learned on this particular field of conflict—that the moment of turning one's back on an enemy who seems safely defeated, and is defeated, is the most dangerous moment of all. And that there can be no guarantees.

LYNDA K. BUNDTZEN

Women in The Bell Jar:
Two Allegories

I. THE ALLEGORY OF THE DOUBLE STANDARD

The structure of *The Bell Jar* is more like a Chinese box than a linear narrative with a distinct beginning, middle, and end in their proper order. Plath begins with the outward circumstances of Esther's depression—her reactions to New York City, the Rosenberg trial, new acquaintances, and her job as a college editor of *Mademoiselle* magazine—and then moves inward and backward in time, revealing incidents from the past that are presumably related to Esther's anxiety. This Chinese box mode of development is exemplified by Esther's progressive recognition of her isolation from other people and in her regression back to the time of her father's death. Her suicide attempt is a further regression; it is depicted as a retreat into the womb and nonentity. While there is considerable overlap and interdependence of the social, artistic, and psychological allegories, their development is similarly like that of a Chinese box. Plath begins with social oppression—the limitations on Esther's future ambitions because she is a woman—moving to the specific threats against her creativity by friends and relatives, to, finally, the ways in which she victimizes herself. This multilayered, self-enclosed form works very well for allegory, each box as a separate episode with a lesson attached to it, and to articulate the movement of Esther's consciousness. In this movement, there are many missing links between episodes, but it is downward and inward to the single hope that the puzzle has been solved,

From *Plath's Incarnations: Women and the Creative Process.* © 1983 by the University of Michigan Press. The sections reprinted here constitute only a fragment of a larger chapter. Later in her book Ms. Bundtzen severely criticizes and qualifies what she says here.

the last box has been opened, and she may crawl in and extinguish her pain. After the suicide attempt, there is a reversal of this process. Esther reaches out first to an inmate at the asylum who is catatonic, and gradually ventures outward again.

Together, the first two episodes of *The Bell Jar* are an allegory about the divided image of woman that emerges from the double standard. Esther's companions are Doreen and Betsy, the stereotypical "bad" girl and "nice" girl of this social ideology. Esther plays each part in turn, both unsuccessfully. This temporary adoption of alternative identities is also one of the major structuring devices of the novel. All of the female characters are doubles for Esther—possible roles she tries on and then discards, because they do not fit her self and because her own sense of self is so fragmented. This desire to be someone else is primarily a form of escape from a feeling of fraudulence and failure.

> All my life I'd told myself studying and reading and writing and working like mad was what I wanted to do, and it actually seemed to be true, I did everything well enough and got all A's, and by the time I made it to college nobody could stop me . . . and now I was apprenticed to the best editor on an intellectual fashion magazine, and what did I do but balk and balk like a dull cart horse.
>
> I wondered why I couldn't go the whole way doing what I should anymore. This made me sad and tired. Then I wondered why I couldn't go the whole way doing what I shouldn't . . . and this made me sadder and more tired.

In the orgy with Doreen and then at the *Ladies' Day* banquet with Betsy, Esther first tries to "go the whole way doing what I shouldn't" and then "the whole way doing what I should." The "bad" girl Doreen is sophisticated, bored, sexy, and representative of a "marvelous, elaborate decadence" that draws Esther "like a magnet." Doreen's "perpetual sneer" at the other girls and their lack of worldly wisdom attracts Esther, who is equally incapable of responding with energy and enthusiasm to her "golden opportunity." The "nice" girl Betsy, on the other hand, is the ingenue—a pure, corny, all-American girl from Kansas, intent on saving Esther from Doreen's influence. Betty co-ed. She is the "should" for Esther, and Betsy wants marriage, a big farm, and lots of children. Betsy will be rewarded for her conformity later by becoming a "model" matron in B. H. Wragge advertisements—a media image for every woman's aspirations. As polar opposites, Doreen and Betsy represent the successful vamp and the future homemaker, and Esther, at least for awhile, envies each of the girls for the security of their identities.

Doreen's wise cynicism, however, evaporates when she is in the presence of a man, and she transforms herself into a tawdry little sex goddess—a diminutive version of Marilyn Monroe. She permits herself to be squeezed and touched by the cowboy disc jockey, Lenny, while pretending not to notice: "She just sat there, dusky as a bleached-blond Negress in her white dress, and sipped daintily at her drink." As Doreen sits there being stared at and fondled, Esther, now alias Elly Higginbottom, does all the talking and tries to sound as worldly as Doreen does when she isn't with a man. At the beginning of the evening, Esther even feels like Doreen—"wise and cynical as all hell"—but as the evening progresses Esther finds herself fading into a shadow-self: "It was so dark in the bar I could hardly make out anything except Doreen. With her white hair and white dress she was so white she looked silver. I think she must have reflected the neons over the bar. I felt myself melting into the shadows like the negative of a person I'd never seen before in my life." There is something enviable about Doreen's total passivity as a sex object, but the Doreen identity fails because it does not give Esther the rebellious feeling of release she hoped for. Plath's comparison of Doreen to a Negress, with its connotations of slavery, tells the reader that she is nothing but a sexual possession. It was the combination of witty sarcasm and decadent sexual experience in Doreen that promised independence and superiority. Without her sneer and her wit, Doreen looks like a "great white macaw" with beautiful plumage but a birdbrain—a stereotypically dumb blond.

Although it is Doreen who passes out in her own vomit before Esther's door, Esther is the one who feels dirtied by the experience of watching Lenny's seduction and Doreen's sexual teasing. She ritualistically bathes after returning to the hotel, and the next day says, "I still expected to see Doreen's body lying there in a pool of vomit like an ugly concrete testimony to my own dirty nature." And, in fact, Esther regurgitates what Doreen represents as unwholesome: "I made a decision about Doreen that night. I decided I would watch her and listen to what she said, but deep down I would have nothing at all to do with her. Deep down, I would be loyal to Betsy and her innocent friends. It was Betsy I resembled at heart."

Innocence, however, proves equally unwholesome. In the next episode, Esther attends a lavish banquet at the promotional expense of *Ladies' Day* magazine. With Betsy, she enters the world of the homemaker, with its helpful hints on cleaning and cooking, new recipes, and "peach-pie" faces of contented domesticity. Nothing could be more hygienic than the spread put out for the guest editors as a "small sample of the hospitality" of the Food Testing Kitchens at *Ladies' Day*. The feast, however, proves to be "chock-full of ptomaine." Esther's attempt to "go the whole way doing what she should" with Betsy, like her attempt to play the bad girl with Doreen, ends with nausea and a sickening vision of the appetizing but poisonous kitchens at *Ladies' Day*.

> I had a vision of the celestially white kitchens of *Ladies' Day* stretching into infinity. I saw avocado pear after avocado pear being stuffed with crabmeat and mayonnaise and photographed under brilliant lights. I saw the delicate, pink-mottled claw meat poking seductively through its blanket of mayonnaise and the bland yellow pear cup with its rim of alligator-green cradling the whole mess.
>   Poison.

The neon and silver seduction of Doreen is nothing compared to this deadly cuteness. The images suggest a sickeningly coquettish domesticity. The crab claws poke above the mayonnaise like a coy woman peeping over a blanket, and the avocado holds its poison lovingly like a mother cradling a baby.

In this comic-book feminist allegory, girls like Betsy are rewarded with marriage, while girls like Doreen, who willingly give men their bodies without marriage, eventually end up empty-handed. This is the lesson Esther learns from her experience. To round off these first two episodes, Esther and Betsy attend a movie based on that moral: "Finally I could see the nice girl was going to end up with the nice football hero and the sexy girl was going to end up with nobody, because the man named Gil had only wanted a mistress and not a wife all along and was now packing off to Europe on a single ticket." We can be thankful that it is precisely at this moment that the ptomaine overwhelms Esther and she has the urge to puke, but the nausea over this wholesome fare is also a signal that Esther cannot share in the innocent naiveté of Betsy, or, as she says later, in scornful Doreen tones, the stupid simplicity of "Pollyanna Cowgirl."

What she cannot, quite literally, swallow is the limitation imposed on her by a double standard and the sexual hypocrisy permitted men in this arrangement. When Esther's mother sends the *Reader's Digest* article "In Defense of Chastity," Esther refuses to accept "the main point" of her culture's sexual arrangements: "that a man's world is different from a woman's world and a man's emotions are different from a woman's emotions and only marriage can bring the two worlds and the two sets of emotions together properly." Instead, she decides that justice demands a quid pro quo.

> I couldn't stand the idea of a woman having to have a single pure life and a man being able to have a double life, one pure and one not.
>
> Finally I decided that if it was so difficult to find a red-blooded intelligent man who was still pure by the time he was twenty-one I might as well forget about staying pure myself and marry somebody who wasn't pure either. Then when he started to make my life miserable I could make his miserable as well.

One of Esther's chief preoccupations is how she can sidestep the rigors of the double standard without becoming a Doreen. Yet every man she meets seems to think of women in these terms. The male imagination in *The Bell Jar* has room for only the pure and the impure. Her college friend Eric tells her that "if he loved anybody he would never go to bed with her. He'd go to a whore if he had to and keep the woman he loved free of all that dirty business." Esther considers Eric a likely candidate for spoiling her purity until he tells her that she reminds him of his older sister, "so I knew it was no use, I was the type he would never go to bed with." In New York, Esther is fixed up with a malevolent version of Eric—the Peruvian woman-hater Marco. He, too, divides women into Madonnas and whores. He is in love with his first cousin, a pure beauty who intends to be a nun, and as if guessing Esther's secret purpose, treats her as a slut, flinging her into the mud and threatening to rape her.

Despite her best efforts, Esther remains "pure" until the end of the novel. It is important to note that the origins of Esther's obsession with purity are presented as social.

> When I was nineteen, pureness was the great issue.
>
> Instead of the world being divided up into Catholics and Prot-estants or Republicans and Democrats or white men and black men or even men and women, I saw the world divided into people who had slept with somebody and people who hadn't, and this seemed the only significant difference between one person and another.

For a young woman, the great social division is between girls who "do" and girls who "don't." Esther's perception of her culture is not a distortion. It is confirmed later by Esther's benefactor, Philomena Guinea, who is willing to help Esther as long as her problem, it is implied, isn't an illegitimate pregnancy.

> My mother said that Mrs. Guinea had sent her a telegram from the Bahamas, where she read about me in a Boston paper. Mrs. Guinea had telegrammed, "Is there a boy in the case?"
>
> If there was a boy in the case, Mrs. Guinea couldn't, of course, have anything to do with it.
>
> But my mother had telegrammed back, "No, it is Esther's writing. She thinks she will never write again."

Ironically, Esther's "purity" saves her from a state institution, and her loss of it later will help to cure her. All of this may seem to be an exaggeration of the issue on Plath's part, except that the first question newspaper reporters asked when Plath herself attempted suicide was whether there was a boy involved in the case [according to Edward Butscher].

II. THE ALLEGORY OF FEMALE CREATIVITY

The allegory of the double standard gives way to and is complicated by Esther's relationship with Buddy Willard. In recompense for the ptomaine, *Ladies' Day* distributes a volume of short stories to the victims. One of them applies to Esther's vendetta against Buddy. It is about a "Jewish man and a beautiful dark nun" who meet at a fig tree growing between the man's house and a convent,

> until one day they saw an egg hatching in a bird's nest on a branch of the tree, and as they watched the little bird peck its way out of the egg, they touched the back of their hands together, and then the nun didn't come out to pick figs with the Jewish man anymore but a mean-faced Catholic kitchen maid came to pick them instead and counted up the figs the man picked after they were both through to be sure he hadn't picked anymore than she had, and the man was furious.

The Edenic innocence of the love between the Jewish man and nun is symbolized by the fruit and the baby bird. The maid's entry, which is like that of the serpent in the garden, introduces lust, jealousy, and small-mindedness. The story reminds Esther of her relationship to Buddy and a similarly blighted innocence and disillusionment with sex: "We had met together under our own imaginary fig tree, and what we had seen wasn't a bird coming out of an egg, but a baby coming out of a woman, and then something awful happened and we went our separate ways." In this little allegory, the kitchen maid is both the waitress with whom Buddy has an affair and Esther, who keeps a balance sheet on sexual encounters. Like the kitchen maid who counts figs to make sure everything is even, Esther is determined that Buddy will not remain one up on her. We discover that Esther is not chafing under the oppression of a double standard so much as she is outraged by Buddy's new power over her. In the past, she basked in the sexual sophistication Buddy told her she had.

> From the first night Buddy Willard kissed me and said I must go out with a lot of boys, he made me feel I was much more sexy and experienced than he was and that everything he did like hugging and kissing and petting was simply what I made him feel like doing out of the blue, he couldn't help it and didn't know how it came about.
>
> Now I saw he had only been pretending all this time to be so innocent. . . .
>
> What I couldn't stand was Buddy's pretending I was so sexy and he was so pure, when all the time he'd been having an affair with that tarty waitress and must have felt like laughing in my face.

Esther feels duped into a false confidence in her sexual attractiveness and potent femininity. The balance of power in their relationship has shifted from an uneasy equality (while Buddy may effectively have put down the impracticality of Esther's artistic ambitions, she could assert her sexual dominance) to a situation where Esther is clearly bested by Buddy's experience.

Her feeling of inferiority is compounded by Buddy's already mentioned exhibition of his genitals—she has never "seen" a man before, only statues, she says—and even more seriously by her attendance with Buddy at the birth of a child. What she sees is another instance of male control over women.

> I was so struck by the sight of the table where they were lifting the woman I didn't say a word. It looked like some awful torture table, with these metal stirrups sticking up in mid-air at one end and all sorts of instruments and wires and tubes I couldn't make out properly at the other.
>
> The woman's stomach stuck up so high I couldn't see her face or the upper part of her body at all. She seemed to have nothing but an enormous spider-fat stomach and two little ugly spindly legs propped in the high stirrups, and all the time the baby was

being born she never stopped making this unhuman whooing noise.

Later Buddy told me the woman was on a drug that would make her forget she'd had any pain and that when she swore and groaned she really didn't know what she was doing because she was in a kind of twilight sleep. . . .

I thought it sounded just like the sort of drug a man would invent.

I didn't feel up to asking if there were any other ways to have babies. For some reason the most important thing to me was actually seeing the baby come out of you yourself and making sure it was yours. I thought if you had to have all that pain anyway you might just as well stay awake.

I had always imagined myself hitching up on to my elbows on the delivery table after it was all over—dead white, of course, with no makeup and from the awful ordeal, but smiling and radiant, with my hair down to my waist, and reaching out for my first little squirmy child and saying its name, whatever it was.

The problem, as Plath dramatizes it here, is that men have usurped the privilege of giving birth from women. The doctors are all male and they are entirely responsible for the emergence of a new creature into the world. To Esther's mind, they have deprived the woman of her consciousness of both the pain and pleasure of birth and used her body for their own purposes, their own ends. The woman and her baby are their opus, their engineering feat. The mother has been made mindless with drugs invented by men, incapable of seeing or comprehending the birth of her own child. Esther, too, is deprived of that vision of herself as a strong woman, enjoying the powers of her own body.

Ultimately, this episode becomes part of the allegory on female creativity in *The Bell Jar*. Men take over women's powers and use them for their own pleasure. Such is the lesson Esther learns in watching a birth and it is reiterated in a second episode, while she is on another date with Buddy.

Once when I visited Buddy I found Mrs. Willard braiding a rug out of strips of wool from Mr. Willard's old suits. She'd spent weeks on that rug, and I had admired the tweedy browns and greens and blues patterning the braid, but after Mrs. Willard was through, instead of hanging the rug on the wall the way I would have done, she put it down in place of her kitchen mat, and in a few days it was soiled and dull and indistinguishable from any mat you could buy for under a dollar in the five and ten.

And I knew that in spite of all the roses and kisses and restaurant dinners a man showered on a woman before he married her, what he secretly wanted was for her to flatten out underneath his feet like Mrs. Willard's kitchen mat.

Esther's little allegory here may be interpreted in sexual terms. This is only one more instance of sex being associated with filth in *The Bell Jar:* Esther's ritualistic bathing to cleanse herself after the orgy with Doreen; Eric's disgust over the dirty surroundings of his sexual initiation by a prostitute; Marco's attempted rape of Esther in a muddy ditch; Irwin's shower after "deflowering" Esther; and here the analogy between the marital relationship and a man wiping his feet on a doormat. But there is also an allegory about the abuse of female creative powers in this incident. Mrs. Willard gleans the materials of her art from clothes cast aside by her husband, but once she transforms them into something beautiful, they return to male use. The moral is as old as the cliché, "You treat me like your personal doormat, and I let you step all over me." The woman acquiesces in her own slavery.

From what she has seen, Esther fears that marriage will destroy her desire to write, that her artistic energies will be channelled into the humdrum activities of a housewife: "I also remembered Buddy Willard saying in a sinister, knowing way that after I had children I would feel differently, I wouldn't want to write poems anymore. So I began to think maybe it was true that when you married and had children it was like being brainwashed, and afterward you went about numb as a slave in some private, totalitarian state." Esther's fears are confirmed by Mrs. Willard's homely wisdom: "'What a man wants is a mate and what a woman wants is infinite security,' and 'What a man is is an arrow into the future and what a woman is is the place the arrow shoots off from.'" But Esther wants "to shoot in all directions myself, like the colored arrows from a Fourth of July rocket." Her mother, too, warns Esther that

nobody wanted a plain English major. But an English major who knew shorthand was something else again. Everybody would want her. She would be in demand among all the up-and-coming young men and she would transcribe letter after thrilling letter.

The trouble was, I hated the idea of serving men in any way. I wanted to dictate my own thrilling letters.

Servitude, brainwashing, numbness, drugs that wipe the mind clear, shock treatments—all of these are closely associated in Esther's mind with the connubial state and its threat to her creativity. Later, this victimization is made a part of her experience as a mental patient, and a bell jar that descends over all women, suspending them forever in a state of arrested development, like "the big glass bottles full of babies that had died before they were born" at Buddy's medical school. The women she meets at the mental asylum are analyzed and given insulin injections, shock treatments, or lobotomies, depending, it seems, on the degree of their rebelliousness. Mrs. Savage appears to have committed herself for no better reason than to "louse up" her daughters' debutante parties with the public shame of a crazy mother. As they get better, the women return to their old lives, filled with shopping and bridge, unfaithful husbands and catty chitchat. In fact, the society of women at Belsize reminds Esther of the "normal" girls in her college dormitory: "What was there about us, in Belsize, so different from the girls playing bridge and gossiping and studying in the college to which I would return? Those girls, too, sat under bell jars of a sort." The nurses and inmates respond with the same envy and excitement at the news of a male visitor and amuse themselves in the same ways. Their docility is symbolized by the lobotomized Valerie, who apparently passes her confinement in complete contentment, watching other women come and go, not so much as a mental patient but as a prim old "Girl Scout Leader" watching her "girls" grow up and leave childish things. Occasionally, there is a pathetic display of creativity and independent spirit: Dee Dee composes a tune on the piano and "everybody kept saying she ought to get it published, it would be a hit." But female society in *The Bell Jar*, whether it's the Amazon Hotel in New York City (an obvious, but clever transformation of the Barbizon for women), a college dormitory, or a mental asylum, is a state of waiting for the "right" man to come along and time is passed with "harem" activities.

Esther is surrounded by women like dolls, zombies, and mannequins. The epitome of this condition is Hilda, another guest editor in New York. She is a mindless mannequin for the stylish hats and other accessories she creates in accord with shifts in fashion (another example of female creative energy channeled into a socially acceptable, and absurdly insignificant, activity). Her narcissistic habit of gazing at herself in shop windows is compensation for nonentity: "she stared at her reflection in the glassed shop windows to make sure, moment by moment, that she continued to exist." Behind her "vacant, Slavic expression" is a "blind cave." She does not, in fact, exist, except for a cavernous voice that reminds Esther of a dybbuk when she responds to Esther's pity for the Rosenbergs: "It's awful such people should be alive. . . . I'm so glad they're going to die." As Esther falls deeper into depression, she comes to resemble Hilda. She is surprised by her reflection in mirrors, as if an unknown "other," flattened out and distorted by the mirror's flaws, stares back. She later sees her suicide like the Rosenbergs' trial and execution as a lurid newspaper headline, and similar to Hilda, is curiously detached from the human pain.

The electrocution of the Rosenbergs is at first simply a recognizable feature in the novel's American landscape. Eventually, Esther's obsession with their case is linked to the shock treatment she is given, which she does not see as therapy, but as a punishment for some terrible, unknown crime.

> Then something bent down and took hold of me and shook me like the end of the world. Whee-ee-ee-ee-ee, it shrilled, through an air crackling with blue light, and with each flash a great jolt drubbed me till I thought my bones would break and the sap fly out of me like a split plant.
>
> I wondered what terrible thing it was that I had done.

It is as if God bent down to smite her. Esther wants to confess to a priest, to be cleansed of her sins, and at one point, even thinks of entering a nunnery; but she has no idea what her "sins" are. Later she tells her nervous Unitarian minister, who has come to call on her in the mental asylum, that she believes in hell. She must live in it before she dies, she says, "to make up for missing out on it after death," and this is a punishment, in turn, for not believing in a life after death.

This circular reasoning is symptomatic of Esther's anxiety and is similar to Freud's description of patients in "Analysis Terminal and Interminable," who, out of an unconscious sense of guilt, punish themselves by never getting well. It is an inner inhibition (i.e., they do not consciously reject health). Likewise, we begin to suspect that Esther's sudden halt after years of accomplishment is motivated by guilt, rather than the opposite cause-effect sequence. It is guilt that leads to failure, rather than, as we normally expect, failure that leads to guilt. And this unusual process of self-victimization casts doubt on both the allegories of the double standard and female creativity as the sole explanations for Esther's depression and her feelings of inadequacy.

SUSAN VAN DYNE

Fueling the Phoenix Fire:
The Manuscripts of Sylvia Plath's
"Lady Lazarus"

Sylvia Plath turned thirty on October 27, 1962. During that week she composed eleven poems. The monumental "Lady Lazarus" was alone among them in being revised over a period of six days. "Lady Lazarus" looms large among the major poems from the last five months of Plath's life which we now regard as her poetic coming of age. These poems are almost obsessively concerned with the making of a literary alter ego—how to realize through language a new vision of the self. In "Lady Lazarus" the poet worried not only about how she would define the self but how she would defend it.

One of the poems conceived around her birthday, "Lady Lazarus" marks the poet's taking stock of her history. Her urge to reorder her past retrospectively and to utter a compelling prophecy about her future prompt this poem's terrifying self-dramatization. A poet who compulsively measured her achievements against others, Plath may well have dreaded her thirtieth birthday. She and her husband had separated during the summer, and she had remained with her two young children in Devon while he returned to London. In July, August, and September she'd written only six poems. For a time, her life seemed to dominate her art and paralyze the forces necessary to create poetry. Yet in the October poems Plath began to reconstruct a persona that was often volatile, violent, and sometimes overbearing in its egotism. She recognized in the aftermath of her marriage that she'd gained access to molten strata of unknown poetic power. She wrote, feverishly, to her mother on October 16 to claim she was ready "to make a new life. I am

From *The Massachusetts Review* 24, no. 2 (Summer 1983). © 1983 by The Massachusetts Review, Inc.

a writer. . . . I am a genius of a writer; I have it in me. I am writing the best poems of my life; They will make my name" [quoted from *Letters Home*].

Now that scholars have access to the manuscripts from this period through the Sylvia Plath Collection at Smith College, we need to re-examine the nature of the relationship between Plath's biography and the poems that made her name. As critics we have created an overly neat, and probably false, dichotomy between Plath's early work in *The Colossus* period, which seems laboriously crafted and intellectually derived from literary models, and her later poems from the *Ariel* period, which appear to be, by contrast, an unmediated transcription of life. What the manuscripts for the *Ariel* poems reveal is unequivocal proof that although the events of Plath's life may have prompted the need for these poems, her characters and narratives were realized through a series of self-conscious, calculated artistic choices. While we are able to note, at many places in the drafts, correspondences between the emerging poem and its underlying personal history, the rearrangements, condensations, and distortions of persons and events in the dream work of the poem hold much more significance. In the manuscripts for the *Ariel* poems we begin to see as well that Plath's relationship to her personal history was no more vexed than her relationship to her literary past. We recognize a woman writer who struggles to conceive of her life outside of the conventional inherited stories that pretend to describe it. Because Plath's late poems are uniformly more daring in the narratives she borrows and subverts in order to make her inward life visible, they enable us to appreciate their resemblance to the fantastic reorderings of Anne Sexton, the Brontës, and Emily Dickinson. In addition, they should cause us to revalue her intentional divergence from the more literal confessions of Robert Lowell.

"Lady Lazarus" is one of the most Gothic of the lot. The poem means to give offense; it makes outrageous claims. One of these is the female persona's appropriation of the suffering of concentration camp inmates as a suitable analogy for the domestic tragedy of a failed marriage. This poem shows us Plath testing her authority, her myth-making capability, exercising a bold new voice that affronts and astonishes. Yet one of Lady Lazarus's strengths is her self-irony; she is as much aware of her excesses as her creator is in this description for a planned BBC broadcast: "The speaker is a woman who has the great and terrible gift of being reborn. The only trouble is she has to die first. She is the phoenix, the libertarian spirit, what you will. She is also just a good, plain, very resourceful woman" [quoted by M. L. Rosenthal in *The Art of Sylvia Plath*, ed. Charles Newman]. In her final months the resourceful woman poet pushed her literary self-conception steadily toward mythic representations that would transfigure or redeem her suffering in extraordinary ways.

Her journals suggest that Plath had always expected her life to be a fabulous story. As a young writer she was determined to master the formulaic fictions of women's magazines. Her fixation with imitating these stories successfully seems at times to govern the paradigms through which she perceived her own experience. Her ambition to be recognized as an artist and her expectation of womanly fulfillment reflect the conventions of popular art like an incongruous cartoon. Anticipating her birthday three years earlier, Plath records in her journal a dream in which "Marilyn Monroe appeared to me . . . as a kind of fairy godmother. . . . She gave me an expert manicure. . . . She invited me to visit her during the Christmas holidays, promising a new, flowering life."

But when she faced the end of her marriage in the summer of 1962, her lifescript threatened to turn into soap opera. Plath refused to play the pitiful roles of betrayed wife or abandoned mother. "What the person out of Belsen—physical or psychological—wants," she wrote her mother just before beginning "Lady Lazarus," "is nobody saying the birdies still go tweet-tweet, but the full knowledge that somebody else has been there and knows the *worst,* just what it is like. It is much more help for me, for example, to know that people are divorced and go through hell, than to hear about happy marriages. Let the *Ladies Home Journal* blither about *those*" (*Letters,* October 21, 1962). The old fictions had failed her. In "Lady Lazarus" she borrowed the miracle of Lazarus, the myth of the phoenix, the hype of the circus, and the horror of the holocaust to prophesy for herself a blazing triumph over her feelings of tawdriness and victimization.

What emerges strikingly when we examine her drafts are the persona's oscillations between feelings of control and powerlessness. We recover, too, a fuller awareness that Plath's reconstructed identity borrows from other stories she'd told about herself—as Esther Greenwood in *The Bell Jar,* as the emerging female alter ego in other poems written in October, most particularly "Stings" and "Ariel," and, in the less obviously fictionalized accounts, as daughter writing letters home to Aurelia Plath and as the self-conscious poet writing and rereading her journals. Her purpose in reshaping these autobiographical sources, as much as her literary sources, was to make available to herself a history she could live with. The history of artistic choices told by these documents individually is impressive enough, but what is most astonishing is that the stories are told in concert, often quite literally superimposed on each other. The Plath Collection, which is housed in Smith's rare book room, contains approximately 4,000 pages of her manuscripts and typescripts, including more than 200 poems in successive drafts, 850 pages of unpublished journals, and 150 annotated volumes from the poet's library.

"Lady Lazarus," like many of the poems from this period, is drafted on used paper. Plath's habit of reusing earlier manuscript material shows a marvellously conserving psychic economy or a reluctance to dispose of good bond paper, or most likely both. During the incredibly productive last two years of her life, she composed on the backs of the final printer's typescript of *The Colossus*, on the reverse of an edited typescript of *The Bell Jar*, used mostly in consecutive order from back to front during October and November, and on scraps of Ted Hughes's poems and plays, which she had originally typed for him. A handwritten six-page draft and the first two typescripts of "Lady Lazarus" all appear on pages from *The Bell Jar*; these are mostly used in sequence, starting with the opening of chapter 3 and running backward through almost all of chapter 2. *The Bell Jar* itself was typed on pink memo paper that Plath acquired when she taught at Smith.

When Plath felt she had a serviceable draft (usually within a single day) she moved to fresh paper for a clean typed version, almost inevitably with a carbon copy. While these typescripts often underwent further editing, Plath usually inscribed them in the upper right corner with her name and address, an encouraging signal to herself that the poems were ready to be mailed to her favorite journals. Often the carbon of the earliest typescript is dated; when revisions occurred over a period of time, she may note dates on the first handwritten draft and subsequent revisions, offering a day-by-day account of their evolution. Fair copies of a completed poem might subsequently be used as scrap when she began composing another poem several months later. Late in January Plath borrowed the back of the first typed copy of "Lady Lazarus" that was on clean bond and had been identified with her name and Devon address to begin composing "Totem" and "Bald Madonnas" (eventually "The Munich Mannequins").

What caused this endless turnover in the poet's paper supply? From her own dated lists, we know that she sent batches of poems out weekly from just after the composition of the sequence of bee poems during early October until a week before her death in early February. Because many of the same poems were recirculated to several different magazines, Plath was certain to have multiple fair copies of the final version on hand ready to go out or being returned in the mail. Yet Plath's habits were clearly prompted by more than convenience. The palimpsestic accretion of the poet's reinscribed manuscripts gives unexpected clues to the evolution of her personal symbol system. In all likelihood, Plath reused a particular page of manuscript because she had been rereading it, either to wonder why a group of poems had been returned or, in the case of the safely published *Colossus* and *Bell Jar,* to reassure herself of earlier productivity. That Plath returned to rework "Lady Lazarus" over a period of six days is significant. In only a few poems from these weeks in October, such as the powerful pivotal poem "Stings" in the bee sequence, did Plath make substantive revisions of a stanza or more after the initial draft or two. I think Plath's hesitation about being done with these poems marks her conviction that they were major works. Even more, I believe her prolonged attention to them and the nature of her revisions indicate the materials and areas of feeling she longed to order and control. Reseeing the manuscript evidence in the Collection as literal palimpsests, through which each document testifies twice or more, complicates our sense of their chronological sequence. We begin to know what images freed her genius or what material demanded to be rehearsed in order to free her.

It is entirely clear in the finished poem that one of the poet's primary needs is to believe in her own will as the agency of her resurrection. The persona of the final version is searingly self-confident—a taunting, bitchy phoenix who appears to loathe her earlier incarnations almost as much as she does her present audience. Although the published version of the poem brags that the voracious, terrifying self is unencumbered by her past, the manuscripts reveal the strain of reconstructing a self that could break free of the dependent, derivative definitions linked to the strong male figures in her life. Certain preoccupations that will ultimately find other shapes or be excised altogether in the finished poem appear in the drafts. What is evident throughout the drafts is her fixation on a male figure as the primary audience for her strenuous self-proclamation. Even more clearly than in the published version, the speaker's performance demands and depends on her audience to validate it. As she moves toward the finished version of her protagonist, Plath chooses to shape her as an active, even manipulative, agent who supersedes earlier images of the self as passive, tortured victim. The imaginative reconstruction of her identity is accomplished through an extended, often oblique, process of negative definition. What the speaker wishes to accomplish by sheer force of will is precisely the inversion of what she fears. Rather than be consumed by the fires of sexual jealousy and helpless rage that appear repeatedly in the imagery of the drafts, the speaker wants to separate herself from her fused identity with Hughes, eliminate the threat of his superior position, and finally appropriate his male powers to herself in a consuming gesture of her own fierce territoriality.

Throughout the manuscripts, Plath knows and names her antagonists more clearly than she can conceive of herself as independent of their claims on her: lover, enemy, professor, executioner, priest, torturer, doctor, God, Lucifer. In order to believe in her ability to reconstitute herself imaginatively as a "smiling woman" of thirty, she must dismiss the social constructions of the self which earlier sustained her. Like the Godiva figure in "Ariel," she must slough off the identities provided by the roles she had assumed as student, wife, mother, patient, even attempted suicide, as so much "trash / to annihilate each decade." Such faith didn't come easily to the poet. The hyperbole in the drafts is even more extreme than in the completed poem. In them the repetitiveness of the speaker's assertions of her power to survive each deconstruction of the self speaks more of fear than of easy self-assurance. As Plath works to hone her anger and turn it outward, to tighten the defense of her macabre self-irony in revisions, a consistent pattern emerges. Initially the persona's love is fused with death; ultimately, Lady Lazarus's new life is fueled by hate. The violent fantasy of the poem is informed by the wish to incorporate the forces that threaten to destroy her.

These are the figures that dominate the worksheets. In using Plath's original manuscripts in the Collection, we are constantly aware that these motifs are inscribed over the narrative of *The Bell Jar* that appears on the reverse. Although it is difficult to determine the origins of specific images in a symbolic system as densely interconnected as Plath's, eerie associative links exist between poem and novel in these double-faced documents. In both narratives, the heroine stresses her feelings of entitlement, expressed in a greedy orality. This defensive response seems prompted, more obliquely in the novel than in the poem, by a sense of deprivation caused by the defection of a significant male figure. Also central to both narratives is a necessary purification through which the persona attempts to free herself from old relational bonds.

In the poem, the first and last of the persona's "deaths" recall her abandonment by her father and by her husband twenty years later. Embedded in the chapter from the novel is Plath's remembrance of her grandfather, who served as surrogate when her father died, and his implied promise that this early loss would be repaired by marriage. The pages from chapter 3 of *The Bell Jar* that serve as scrap for the handwritten draft of the poem present the sumptuous *Ladies' Day* luncheon that will later make the heroine Esther Greenwood deathly ill. Eating caviar and avocados reminds her of the "stolen" treats provided by her grandfather when she was nine. The childhood luxury of caviar is not only an implied compensation for the loss of her father, but further, as Esther self-consciously elaborates, "at my wedding my grandfather would see I had all the caviar I could eat. It was a joke because I never intended to get married." Plath tended to lump male disappointments together; here she found reminders of several readily available for reworking in the poem. Even more striking is Esther's sense of her audience at lunch as alien, critical, and competitive. She gorges on the extra caviar to fortify her own feelings of entitlement against the other guests who might demand that she share. In the poem, Lady Lazarus must protect herself from the greedy encroachments of the "peanut-crunching crowd." Finally, the end of the first handwritten draft appears on the reverse of pages from chapter 2 in which Esther enacts a ritual bath purifying herself of all entangling relationships. As troubling men and rival females dissolve away in the bath, Esther proclaims, "I don't know them, I have never known them. [I am a virgin,] and I am very pure." To cleanse her heroine after another decade, Plath would need to subject Lady Lazarus to fire before she can "rise a [bloody] [blooming] [sweet white] virgin." (Note: brackets [ ] in these quotations enclose material deleted by the poet during her revision of a particular draft.)

What is remarkable about Plath's worksheets is the progressive purification the poem undergoes. Her deletions are almost always her most significant choices. Passages which take repeated tinkering often drop away altogether; yet the material worried over in such passages often prompts a key image or word choice that governs a later stage in the poem. I want to focus on two of the most reworked areas in the worksheets to demonstrate how a woman artist reshaped cultural stories in order to transmute personal autobiography into more public poetic myth. In order to re-imagine her heroine, Plath first had to probe the nature of her dependence on the male figures through whom she had previously defined herself. With the defection of Hughes and the end of their marriage, several of Plath's most elaborately maintained stories about her identity as woman and poet were threatened at once. In her letters and journals she often proposes the analogy that her poetry represented an excess of her natural fertility. She believed her poems would confirm and extend her procreative powers as child-bearer. Although she was widely published in magazines before she ever bore children, she rejoiced that the birth of her daughter Frieda marked the spring and the publication of her first book *The Colossus* marked the fall of the same year. She was convinced that her poetic fruitfulness would be rooted in her experience of motherhood.

Significantly, the Lazarus story was linked in Plath's associations with barrenness. In April of 1956, in the flush of Hughes' courtship, she boasted to her mother of the perfect integration of her life with Ted and her work as a poet: "My voice is taking shape, coming strong. Ted says he never read poems by a woman like mine; they are strong and full and rich . . . they are working, sweating, heaving poems born out of the way words should be

said." She compared her full devotion to Ted with total self-knowledge and
fulfillment: "Although I am using every fiber of my being to love him, even
so, I am true to the essence of myself, and I know who that self is . . . I know
this with a sure strong knowing to the tips of my toes, and having been on the
other side of life like Lazarus, I know that my whole being shall be one song
of affirmation and love all my life long" (*Letters*, April 29, 1956). Clearly,
to be Lazarus was to doubt such integration and affirmation. Three years
later in Boston, Plath connected Lazarus to an idea for a short story. She felt
her life was stalled. Working part-time at Massachusetts General Hospital
writing up mental patients' case histories, she despaired of her ability to
produce poems or to generate characters or plots substantial enough for a
novel. In the same period she berated herself for her inability to become
pregnant, believing she was infertile and therefore fatally flawed as a woman.
The seed for a story called "Lazarus My Love" was noted in her journals as
a startling "Comeback from the dead. Kicking off thermometers" erupting
in the "violent ward" of the mental hospital.

In fall of 1962 Plath needed to manage her own comeback after suffering the death of her chosen self-image as the perfect intellectual and
biological partner for Hughes. In the drafts for "Lady Lazarus" the strains
of separating her identity from his are everywhere apparent. With intense
ambivalence, the speaker regards a male figure whom she must identify,
within the same breath, as her greatest love and her greatest enemy. In the
third stanza, she struggles to claim her separate reality in the face of this confounding fusion. The encounter is one of the most heavily reworked passages
in the poem:

> Peel off the napkin
>
> [My] [Great] Love, [my] [great] enemy.
>
> [It is certainly I] Do I terrify?
>
> Yes [yes] Yes Herr Professor
>
> [It is I] I is I
>
> Can [You] you [cannot] deny
>
> The nose, the eye pits, the full set of teeth?

Her sense of herself seems to depend here on gaining recognition from the
other. Her anxious assertions demand confirmation, but she seems to expect

only denial. She presents herself as Hughes's bad ghost, the walking corpse he can't walk out on.

In this scenario, who does he become? Throughout the handwritten draft the antagonism between them is intimate and pervasive. Whenever the poet invokes his presence in this fused image of lover/enemy, she releases a rush of affect that temporarily takes over the poem and that she chooses consistently later to delete. She imagines the speaker locked into a hellish cycle of aggression and recrimination with a male antagonist. She smoulders in the fires of sexual jealousy and thwarted rage, vowing that she'll emerge from the forge renewed and even more dangerous to her torturer:

> [so love], [so] enemy
>
> I burn & turn
>
> So, Herr Enemy
>
> You age, & I am new.
>
> I am the baby/on/your/anvil./I eat fire
>
> . . . .
>
> You say I am dangerous
>
> I burn & turn & have no need for you.
>
> Well yes, I guess
>
> I am very dangerous [when it comes to you!]
>
> Very, very dangerous, when it comes to you!

These fires resemble the feverish purgation of sexual passion and rejection of her lover in "Fever 103°" written less than a week earlier. The evidence of these passages suggests that even to name the male figure as "love" proved too dangerous artistically for Plath. In order to see herself safely separate from him, the poet had to find cooler terms.

In her revisions, Plath substitutes epithets that would seem to entitle him to enviable positions of power and dominance: "Herr Professor," "Herr Doktor," "Herr Enemy," "Herr God," "Herr Lucifer." Yet naming these attributes or roles served to clarify for the poet what her developing heroine lacked, and what Lady Lazarus would need to claim as her own in order to survive. In the process of negative definition which organizes the poem, the association of the male figure with cruelty and authority yields a composite projection of what the speaker both fears and desires. Once appropriately

named, these monolithic male figures apparently freed the poet to stage for
Lady Lazarus a kind of guerilla theatre with her imagined audience in which
their expected roles are systematically reversed. The speaker assaults her
audience with her terrifying self-disclosures. In exhibiting her corpse, she
will teach her former tutor a lesson in brutality; in annihilating the trash
of her earlier selves, she'll prove to the doctor that she can cure herself; in
performing her suicidal act "so it feels like hell," she'll rival Lucifer in her
ability to suffer; and in arranging her own resurrection, she demonstrates
she can do without God's intervention. In reworking the image of the male
figure, the worksheets show a movement from a highly conflicted fusion with
an intimate antagonist toward a defiant separation from stylized, archetypal
representations of male authority. In working out these changes, Plath is able
to eliminate the wordiness of threats such as "we are not done with each
other" and "I am very dangerous when it comes to you" in favor of more
overt intimidation and manipulation of her audience.

In reconstructing Lady Lazarus as a survivor rather than a compulsive
suicide, Plath needed to try out several alternative visions of the heroine in
the worksheets. In defining her character, probably the most important decision was choosing her voice. Except perhaps for the daughter in "Daddy,"
none of Plath's speakers is more determinedly unpleasant, more deserving of
the predictable female pejorative, shrill. Her analogies are intentionally pre-
sumptuous, her flippant colloquialisms are knowingly in poor taste. Plath's
control of voice is Lady Lazarus's chief defense for keeping the peanut-
crunching crowd at bay. But this abrasive self-presentation is not uniformly
present in the worksheets. In fact we can chart the evolution of Plath's new
heroine in the passages whose tone is noticeably unlike the final poem. Given
the brittle self-irony that distinguishes Lady Lazarus as carnival barker and
suicidal stuntwoman, it's surprising to discover in the drafts several passages
in which she speaks with unguarded vulnerability. The first is an extended
image of the recovered suicide as a martyred saint:

> I am supple, I breathe gently
>
> And shall sit [here] a[while] little, [uncommon] [on
>   this green common]
>
> Loving the death that killed me like a lover.
>
> Now it is over
>
> [And] I am involved & still, a wax madonna

The wax madonna's suffering is passive, even erotically willing; her tone is elegiac rather than acerbic. In her self-involvement she looks toward the grave rather than toward the crowd. This section, which was completely dropped after the first draft, most closely resembles the tranquility of the second suicide attempt which follows a few stanzas later. Describing that womb-like retreat, Plath adds and deletes the word "peaceful" four separate times within the space of two lines.

Just after recalling this event, Plath's speaker in the draft confesses her concern for her children. They are both identified as girls; Plath's apparent formal motive was to rhyme "girls" with "pearls" in the preceding line. Yet what follows this evocation is a touching brief rehearsal of the fairy tale of female fulfillment that had just failed the poet herself so miserably:

> Now I have two girls.
>
> I want to see them rich & married well
>   [comfortable]
>
> They are already beautiful
>
> And are They [are] proud
>
> Of their mum's profession? Yes!
>
> Dying//is an art like everything else.
>
> I do it exceptionally well.

Implicit in this passage is one of the central brooding questions Plath tried to answer in the poems she wrote in October. What is her profession? She jokes, here, that she's had most success as an attempted suicide. Yet what does this vocation suggest about her other chosen role as mother? Furthermore, how has her experience of these two professions altered her definition of the poet as resurrected Lazarus, whose "whole being," she imagined in 1956, would be "one song of affirmation and love all my life long"?

In revising, Plath chose to excise both of these comparatively selfless portraits as uncharacteristic of the Lady Lazarus she now needed to imagine. The next stage in the reconstruction of the heroine is marked by passages whose tone is defensive rather than defenseless. Throughout the handwritten draft are complaints of victimization. These are alike in acknowledging the speaker's ambivalence about whether she chose her deaths or merely submitted to them. In two separate sections, she insists an executioner is a constant presence in these scenes. In an extended passage on the third page of the handwritten draft, the unequal forces arrayed against her include not only the executioner, but "a priest & a torturer," and a hostile "mob." This section is crucial for its evidence of the female persona's lingering feelings of paranoia and powerlessness that are subsequently deleted:

> And there's always [a mob &] an executioner
>
> And a priest & a torturer
>
> And a couple of horses & a wheel to give the crowd
>
> [to give the crowd that] [an extra] its thrill.
>
> The extra kicks [they] it pays for.

Moreover, certain key terms here, "thrill" and "kicks" used to describe the mob's voyeuristic appetite, seem to suggest, several stanzas later, the pivotal term for the last stage in the heroine's transformation.

"Charge" comes to stand for the high-premium, high-voltage exchange between the final incarnation of Lady Lazarus and her audience. Between the deleted passage and what becomes stanza 19 of the finished poem, the balance of power is shifted dramatically from the crowd to the speaker: "There is a charge / For fingering my scars, There is a charge." She sets the price they must pay to see her suffer. But the word itself is charged, I think, with more than this meaning. The former tortured victim clearly intends to demand compensation for her pain; she will even affect a sadistic pleasure in exhibiting it and controlling their response. But, like the crowd, she also seems to get a thrill from the performance. While apparently disdaining their gullibility and voyeurism, the speaker's reactions demonstrate that she feels powerfully the reciprocal charge that flows between actor and observer:

> the same brute
>
> Amused shout:
>
> 'A miracle!'
>
> That really knocks me out.

Finally, in the draft for this section, Plath returns to the intimate nexus of her intended role reversal. In the initial version, the speaker's orchestration of events for which her audience must pay is graphically physical and increasingly personal, from "fingering" her scars, to "stethoscoping" her heart, to the final veiled threat: "And there is a charge, a very large charge / For a [night in my bed]." Recovering this variant causes us to hear again the bitter ironies in the earlier lines "Are they proud / Of their mum's profession?" It also suggests the high cost to the poet of constructing such a callous persona in Lady Lazarus: the versatile stuntwoman who will pose as a saint and barter like a prostitute.

I've suggested the pattern and possible motives I see emerging from the poet's choices to delete and revise her worksheets. From the evidence of the initial handwritten draft, what I have described as stages in the reconstruction of the heroine, and her separation from the male antagonist, were choices made largely within a single day. Plath's instincts were certain and swift during this period of composition. She almost never doubted the beginning impulse for a poem; her dramatic first lines emerge at once and remain untouched. Yet she typically reworked a large section of the final movement of a poem in three or four successive efforts even within the initial draft. The last two-and-a-half pages of this six-page handwritten draft focus on recasting the ending.

Throughout these versions, the struggle to resurrect an image of a powerful, autonomous heroine exists in uneasy tension with the desire to reduce to ashes any remnant of a self derivatively defined by her relationship to Hughes. From what we can recover in the worksheets, the ritual of deconstructing that self resonates against a group of emotionally laden images from the recent and distant past. In "Burning the Letters," a poem written the previous August, Plath tries to purge herself of the accumulated burden of Hughes's correspondence and manuscripts, the record of what she now feels has been a past based on deception. The gestures of this ceremony resemble the imagined cremation of "Lady Lazarus":

> So I poke at the carbon birds in my housedress.
>
> . . . .
>
> With the butt of a rake
>
> I flake up papers that breathe like people
> > ("Burning the Papers," August 13)
>
> Out of that ash
>
> You poked//till it lay in a hush//Without cough
> > or stir
>
> I rise,[to eat the air] with my red hair.
> > (draft for "Lady Lazarus," October 23)

In the second poem, however, the roles are significantly reversed. The effort to purge the past fails in "Burning the Letters" because the name of Ted's lover rises from the ashes to assault the stricken speaker anew. In "Lazarus," it's the male figure who fails in the attempt to incinerate the protean female force and who must witness her fiery ascension.

How her heroine would actually rise from the ashes was not entirely clear to Plath during the poem's gestation. Although her final vision is allied with the mythic phoenix, the worksheets reveal that the conception of this figure is more intimately related to similar images of the reborn self created in Plath's other October poems. In the poet's first effort to bring Lady Lazarus back from the dead, on the second page of the handwritten draft, she is virginal yet unequivocally mortal as well: "Each time I rise, I rise a [bloody] [blooming] [sweet white] virgin." During the same week that Plath was revising this poem, she also composed two others, "Poppies in October" and "Nick and the Candlestick," in which fresh blood "blooms" to remind her of the vitality of love and life. Later, Plath would drop this first image of the rising Lazarus as premature.

Her dramatic resurrection clearly belonged to the final movement of the poem; but even here Plath vacillated between having her come back as a newborn or as a fully-fledged creature. Twice she tries out a set of lines that picture Lazarus as an unkillable infant: "You age, and I am new. / I am the baby / on your anvil, / I eat fire." More appealing, finally, to Plath was the image of her as an avenging female who was both erotically tempting and fearsomely destructive. The fire that threatened to destroy her is reignited in her red hair: "I rise with my red [hair] [terrible, feathery hair] hair / My incendiary feathers, and I eat men like air."

Here the adjective "terrible" echoes the speaker's rhetorical question "Do I terrify?" in stanza three. Equally significant, "terrible" is a key term in the description of the recovered self in "Stings" in which the queen bee rises from apparent death "More terrible than she ever was, red / Scar in the sky, red comet." Interestingly, one of the most memorable images of the speaker in "Stings" is her "dense hair." Plath's composite image of the risen Lady Lazarus seems as much siren as phoenix. What's truly astonishing about the evolution of the heroine is her consistently voracious appetite. She rises "to eat the air." Unscathed by torture, she boasts, "I eat fire." Finally she threatens, "I eat men like air."

The heroine's last gesture underscores the wish driving the entire poem, the wish to appropriate the powers that threaten to destroy her. In moving away from the agonizing fusion with the male antagonist evident in the early stages of the poem, the speaker achieves separation by distancing herself from simplified authoritarian male roles. Through her verbal gestures, however, the speaker attempts to reverse the dominance she identifies with these male figures. By manipulating her audience's responses through her hyperbolic, aggressive self-disclosures, the speaker claims her ability to control the situation, to make good her opening bravado and "manage it." The poet's revenge is to turn the tables on the husband and fellow-poet who, she fears, objectified her as his "opus," his "valuable," his "pure gold baby." Her power is language, the power to name. She invokes as her final witnesses "Herr God" and "Herr Lucifer." She magnifies her opponents in order to make her victory more significant; finally, however, she trivializes them to make it more secure.

The ascension of Lady Lazarus marks one of several attempts to imagine a terrifying new integrity for the poet. Throughout most of the final version of the poem, the persona experiences herself as split. She reports her actions from the dual perspective of actor and observer at once, as in these lines:

> Soon, soon the flesh
>
> The grave cave ate will be
>
> At home on me, and I a smiling woman
>
> or
>
> They had to call & call
>
> And pick the worms off me like sticky pearls.

She is hyper-conscious not only of her own feelings, but of her image in others' eyes. Yet perceiving herself as split, as both subject and object, self and other, may be the last vestige of the alienating male perspective she longs to escape from.

In her last utterance, the speaker claims to have moved outside the orbit of male dominance altogether. But has she? Her efforts to heal the split, to articulate a radical integrity, are noticeably different from the closing visions of other October poems that predict the rebirth of a heroine. In "Ariel" the self-absorbed drive of the speaker is undeniably ecstatic even though it may spell the extinction of the individual self. In "Stings" the rising queen is autonomous; she is liberated from the "stingless dead men" who appear in the drafts but who are unmentioned in the final poem. The close of "Lady Lazarus" is more frightening in its explicit urge for revenge and more fearful in its need for it. In Plath's incandescent image, the phoenix rises in rage. The men that she eats like air fuel that final fire.

MELODY ZAJDEL

Apprenticed in a Bible of Dreams:
Sylvia Plath's Short Stories

Although Sylvia Plath wrote approximately seventy short stories, only ten were published in her lifetime. Since her death, three appeared in popular magazines and an additional seven stories were printed in the recently published volume *Johnny Panic and the Bible of Dreams*. What is interesting to the reader of these twenty stories is the consistency with which Plath dealt with the same materials and themes throughout her fiction. Although her prose works span over ten years, much of that time seems spent in writing and rewriting the same story, the story which reaches its fruition in *The Bell Jar*. This is particularly obvious in several of the short stories published after her death ("Tongues of Stone," "Sweetie Pie and the Gutter Men," and "Johnny Panic and the Bible of Dreams"). These stories, along with "In the Mountains" (published in the *Smith Review*, 1954), serve almost as apprentice pieces for key scenes in *The Bell Jar*, containing episodes with the same actions, characters, images, sometimes even the same words. Beyond these apprentice pieces, however, a reader discovers that not only do Plath's stories stylistically show her direct movement into the writing of *The Bell Jar*, but they also mirror her continued thematic concern with two interrelated ideas: first, the idea of living and sustaining a life of the imagination, and second, the socio-mythic form of this theme, what Josephine Donovan has called "the sexual politics of Sylvia Plath." Although Plath's short stories will probably not change her reputation from poet to proficient popular fiction writer (an epithet that Hughes suggests she desired), they are markers to understanding Plath's skill in her finished fictional effort, *The Bell Jar,* just as *The Colossus* stands as a necessary apprenticeship to the final poems of *Ariel*.

From *Critical Essays on Sylvia Plath*. © 1984 by Linda W. Wagner. G. K. Hall, 1984.

Hughes indicates that Plath "launched herself into *The Bell Jar* in 1960." But at least the four stories mentioned above, written between 1954 and 1959, deal with some of the same material. One in particular, "Tongues of Stone" (1955), uses the experience of a young girl's nervous breakdown much as Plath uses it in *The Bell Jar*. At least six key incidents appear first in this story, before being transformed and interpolated into the novel. The start of the breakdown is the same in both pieces. The main character is suffering from extreme apathy, anxiety and insomnia. In *The Bell Jar*, Esther enters the first clinic, Walton, after three weeks of not sleeping; in "Tongues of Stone," the character is at the end of two months of sleeplessness. In setting the scene, the "Tongues of Stone" narrator explains, "It was sometime in October; she had long ago lost track of all the days and it really didn't matter because one was like another and there were no nights to separate them because she never slept anymore." Both young women try to forestall their depression by looking for intellectual occupations to, literally, kill time. Each tries particularly hard to read, only to find the print on the pages of their books indecipherable, "dead black hieroglyphs" and "fantastic, untranslatable shapes, like Arabic and Chinese." Both are denied solace by their alienation from the dead intellectual world represented by the printed books. But more obvious in their similarities than these parallels of general circumstances are the active steps in their attempted suicides and their subsequent treatments. Looking at these steps, the reader can see Plath's movement from a rather flat narrative to the evocative and powerful personal voice of the novel. The apprentice piece has all the isolated units but doesn't have the developed style, theme or political focus of *The Bell Jar*.

    First, in both "Tongues of Stone" and *The Bell Jar*, each of the girls visits her sleeping mother and comes to an important realization: there is neither parental security nor any meaningful reason to continue being in either the present or the future. In "Tongues of Stone," the main character slips into her mother's bed and, lying beside her, "listen[s] to the thin thread of her mother's breathing, wanting to get up and twist the life out of the fragile throat, to end at once the process of slow disintegration which grinned at her like a death's head everywhere she turned." The girl (who remains nameless throughout the story) has sought out her mother. By getting close to her, the girl hopes to stave off the fears and despair she feels. But the mother can neither solace nor protect her daughter. Asleep, she is even unaware of the girl's presence. She is perceived by her daughter as fragile and disintegrating, not a possible haven or shelter against the death her daughter sees everywhere, even in her. This same incident occurs in *The Bell Jar*, but some of the narrator's feelings have changed. In the novel, the mother is less mutual victim, another fragile throat which can be stopped, and more a despised perpetrator of circumstances, a guardian of the world's values and actions. The main character, Esther, looks at her sleeping mother, listens to her piggish snores, and explains, "for a while it seemed to me that the only way to stop it [the sound in her mother's throat] would be to take the column of skin and sinew from which it rose and twist it to silence between my hands." Not only is the mother more unattractive in this version (being piggish and irritating), but the action of strangling her is not done to stop a mutual disintegration, a slow and painful change, but more to assuage Esther's aggressive dislike of what her mother represents. She and her mother are struggling against one another, tussling between them expectations for Esther's future and Esther's own inchoate desires. Neither is totally passive. Esther views the strangling not as euthanasia, but as a means of effectively changing her own world. Where in "Tongues of Stone" the girl creeps into her mother's bed for solace, in *The Bell Jar* Esther merely looks at her mother from the bedroom door, not seeking communion with a source of safety so much as observing the enemy.

After this scene, both stories show the female protagonist trying to escape the world around her by hiding under the mattress of her bed. In each case, she hopes to be crushed, to never reawaken to the oppressive world of sleepless, meaningless, comfortless living. In "Tongues of Stone," the girl leaves her mother's bed, "Creeping back to her own bed, then, she had lifted up the mattress, wedging herself in the crevices between mattress and bedsprings, longing to be crushed beneath the heavy slab." More immediately, the same scene is enacted in *The Bell Jar:* "I crawled between the mattress and the padded bedstead and let the mattress fall across me like a tombstone. It felt dark and safe under there, but the mattress was not heavy enough. It needed about a ton more weight to make me sleep." In the second scene, the tone is sharper. The slab has been defined as a tombstone, the oppression and death imagery are more overt. Plath's character recognizes consciously what she is seeking (the safe dark of death) and what it would take to achieve it (about a ton more).

Both girls then attempt suicide (actually reach out to take hold of the darkness), but are discovered at the last moment and saved. Upon first awakening from their drugged state, each believes herself blind. In "Tongues of Stone," the narrator explains that

> At first they thought she would be blind in that eye. She had lain
> awake the night of her second birth into the world of flesh, talk-
> ing to a nurse who was sitting up with her, turning her sightless

face toward the gentle voice and saying over and over again, "But I can't see, I can't see."

The nurse, who had also believed that she was blind, tried to comfort her, saying, "There are a lot of other blind people in the world. You'll meet a nice blind man and marry him someday."

In this scene the nurse is an acknowledged presence, someone known and staying *with* the girl, not just beside her. She is described as gentle and comforting, albeit not well-informed. This same scene is recreated in *The Bell Jar,* only this time the nurse's presence is not so immediately felt as sympathetic.

> I opened my eyes.
> It was completely dark.
> Somebody was breathing beside me.
> "I can't see," I said.
> A cheery voice spoke out of the dark. "There are lots of blind people in the world. You'll marry a nice blind man someday."

Although the changes are slight, they do match up with the more sinister and detached feelings of Esther in the novel. The nurse in the second presentation is not known immediately, she is somebody. She is not with the girl, she is beside her. Although she is cheery, unlike the original image of comforting presence, we have no reason to assume her intentions are personal; rather, they smack of habitual, professional cheeriness.

Each girl also tries to strangle herself, although the timing of the attempt varies. In "Tongues of Stone," the girl is in the sanatorium, frustrated and depressed that the insulin treatment is not working. She considers strangulation as a means to end the continuing depression and self-disgust.

> One night she hid the pink cotton scarf from her raincoat in the pillowcase when the nurse came around to lock up her drawers and closet for the night. In the dark she had made a loop and tried to pull it tight around her throat. But always just as the air stopped coming and she felt the rushing grow louder in her ears, her hands would slacken and let go, and she would lie there panting for breath, cursing the dumb instinct in her body that fought to go on living.

In *The Bell Jar*, Esther considers and experiments with strangulation as one possible form of suicide, trying a number before the final attempt with sleeping pills. At first, in her version of the scene, she hopes to hang herself, but finding no adequate beam in the house, she explains,

I sat on the edge of my mother's bed and tried pulling the cord tight.

But each time I would get the cord so tight I could feel a rushing in my ears and a flush of blood in my face, my hands would weaken and let go, and I would be all right again.

Then I saw that my body had all sorts of little tricks, such as making my hands go limp at the crucial second, which would save it, time and again, whereas if I had the whole say, I would be dead in a flash.

In this revised scene, the body's instinctual response is more malevolent; it is not simply "dumb," but it has "all sorts of little tricks." In *The Bell Jar* the character's paranoia and mind-body split is strongly felt. The world is active in its oppression, the body active in its rebellion to the will.

Finally, both stories describe the insulin treatment used to combat the character's suicidal depressions. Each story starts with the appearance of a nurse to administer the insulin injection. In "Tongues of Stone,"

At seven the nurse came in to give the evening insulin shot. "What side?" she asked, as the girl bent mechanically over the bed and bared her flank.

"It doesn't matter," the girl said, "I can't feel them any more."

The nurse gave an expert jab. "My, you certainly *are* black and blue," she said.

In *The Bell Jar*, the characters are both detached as well. The section is a little less calm, however, since we are at least aware of what Esther sees when she views herself.

The nurse gave a little clucking noise. Then she said, "Which side?" It was an old joke.

I raised my head and glanced back at my bare buttocks. They were bruised purple and green and blue from past injections. The left side looked darker than the right.

"The right."

"You name it." The nurse jabbed the needle in, and I winced, savoring the tiny hurt.

It is also useful to note that Esther does feel something in this episode: pain. And that is welcomed, for it is something instead of the dull apathy of the first scene.

The final movement in each story is the breakthrough caused by the girls' reactions to the insulin treatment. In each case, the reaction signals the momentary lifting of the oppressive atmosphere, the depression, and bell jar which each of the characters is laboring under. After what has seemed a fruitless waiting in "Tongues of Stone," a period where even the sun's warmth is absent from the day, the girl's reaction occurs, accompanied by a proliferation of growth and light images.

> In the blackness that was stupor, that was sleep, a voice spoke to her, sprouting like a green plant in the dark.
>
> "Mrs. *Patterson*, Mrs. *Patterson*, Mrs. *Patterson*!" the voice said more and more loudly, rising, shouting. Light broke on seas of blindness. Air thinned.
>
> The nurse Mrs. Patterson came running out from behind the girl's eyes. "Fine," she was saying, "fine, let me just take off your watch so you won't bang it on the bed." . . .
>
> The dark air had thinned and now it lived. There had been the knocking at the gate, the banging on the bed, and now she was saying to Mrs. Patterson words that could begin a world: "I feel different. I feel quite different."
>
> "We have been waiting for this a long time," Mrs. Patterson said, leaning over the bed to take the cup, and her words were warm and round, like apples in the sun. "Will you have some hot milk? I think you'll sleep tonight."
>
> And in the dark the girl lay listening to the voice of dawn and felt flare through every fiber of her mind and body the everlasting rising of the sun.

As the ending of the short story, this scene optimistically portends a healing conclusion. The sun has returned; in fact, it is speaking directly to the girl. Both the blackness she emerges from and the real world (represented by the nurse) are positive; the first is a plant; the second, warm and round as an apple. The air is clear, the light quite literally and figuratively dawns. The girl herself speaks words and listens to a voice which apparently signals the start of a new world. In *The Bell Jar,* the parallel scene follows the same progression, but has a slightly different tone.

> I had fallen asleep after the evening meal.
>
> I was awakened by a loud voice, *Mrs. Bannister, Mrs. Bannister, Mrs. Bannister, Mrs. Bannister.* As I pulled out of sleep, I found I was beating on the bedpost with my hands and calling. The sharp, wry figure of Mrs. Bannister, the night nurse, scurried into view.
>
> "Here, we don't want you to break this."

She unfastened the band of my watch.

"What's the matter? What happened?"

Mrs. Bannister's face twisted into a quick smile. "You've had a reaction."

"A reaction?"

"Yes, how do you feel?"

"Funny. Sort of light and airy."

Mrs. Bannister helped me sit up.

"You'll be better now. You'll be better in no time. Would you like some hot milk?"

"Yes."

And when Mrs. Bannister held the cup to my lips, I fanned the hot milk out on my tongue as it went down, tasting it luxuriously, the way a baby tastes its mother.

In this version of the scene, several things have changed. In "Tongues of Stone," the girl is the first one to focus on the change in both herself and her surroundings. She feels "different" and it is not just her, but the atmosphere, the world, which is light and airy. In *The Bell Jar*, Esther feels "funny," "light and airy." But we have no sense of whether the external world is in accord. In "Tongues of Stone," the girl seems to have become attuned again to the physical, natural world. In *The Bell Jar*, the natural world referred to is that of mother and child, not the most hopeful image when taken in the context of the heavily negative connotations given to that relationship throughout the rest of the novel, both before and after this scene. (Consider, in particular, Esther's own relationship with her mother, her sense of all mothers—hers and Buddy's—as circumscribing her opportunities, the notion that becoming a mother herself would kill her chances to be a writer, a complete person in her own right.)

Obviously, Plath is using the same material, even some of the same phrases and images, in this early story and *The Bell Jar*. Equally obviously, there are some significant differences in her presentations, many of which seem caused by an increased thematic awareness on Plath's part in the novel. In "Tongues of Stone," we have a description more than a clearly delineated conflict. The causes of the breakdown, the fears for the future, the active resistance of the girl to both medical help and her surroundings, are never presented. It seems doubtful that the girl herself is aware of all the factors surrounding her previous actions. We are given a third-person, limited view of the events. All conflicts and conditions leading to the suicide attempt are cloaked. In the expanded scope of *The Bell Jar*, on the other hand, the older Esther, the narrator, has moved to a recognition, frequently frustrated and angry, of the social and familial forces which lead to her breakdown. Her mother is seen in sharply critical relief. Her male doctor is at best indifferent to Esther's struggle; at worst he denies its value. It is a world of stultified options and intellectual sterility which places Esther under the bell jar. It is this thematic awareness even more than a stylistic change which gives *The Bell Jar* a power lacking in the earlier story. This same factor accounts for much of the difference between the other apprentice pieces and the novel.

"In the Mountains" also rehearses a scene for *The Bell Jar*. Isobel, a young college woman, goes to visit her boyfriend, Austin, who has been in a TB sanatorium for six months. (This parallels Esther Greenwood's later visit to Buddy Willard under the same constraints.) Isobel comes to visit, to find an unchanged Austin, "Still strong, she thought, and sure of himself." But she comes also with the awareness that "everything was changed for her," and it is this awareness that she needs to articulate to Austin. In a discussion about marriage in general, their differences are highlighted. Austin implies his desire for a commitment, a marriage, while Isobel, in her newly changed persona, explains that she is not ready to consider such a step. " 'Affairs are one thing,' she said. 'But signing your life away because you're lonely, because you're afraid of being lonely, that's something else again. . . . That's the way I figure it now anyway.' " For the first time in their relationship, Austin is vulnerable and expresses his need for Isobel. But part of his attraction to her is still the result of seeing her as appropriate to be his wife. Austin notes she is attractive, just as his doctor's wife is attractive, just as a doctor's wife should be. He sees her as fitting a role, a role which he needs filled, not necessarily one she *wants* to fill. He recalls all the things they've "been through together," but where they serve to be fond memories for him, Isobel recalls "how it was all so lovely and hurting then. How everything he said had hurt her." Where he is now able to proclaim his need for her, she is no longer as needing of him, nor does he offer her anything beyond his need. In the end, when he reaches out for her, thinking to claim her, she is stricken, immobilized and feels them surrounded by a landscape "hushed and still," frozen and deathlike. In the story, the reader is made aware of the change in Isobel, as we are similarly made aware in *The Bell Jar* of the change in Esther. However, in "In the Mountains," there is less overt understanding of the cause of Isobel's change. The novel form allows Plath to finally put all the isolated scenarios together, to juxtapose them until the common conflicts become clear. Esther's rejection of Buddy is more clearly a rejection of not just the individual, but also the prescribed role which her relationship to Buddy (as his future wife) threatens to lock her into. Likewise, the almost malicious pleasure that Buddy feels when Esther breaks her leg (and thus becomes less threatening, less independent) is missing from the short story.

In the story, the reader can still pity Austin, if only slightly; in the novel, Plath gives us little option to disliking Buddy almost as much as Esther does because we see the large issues capitulation to his vulnerability and vision would represent.

In "Sweetie Pie and the Gutter Men," Myra Wardle, a young, childless, married woman who has lately "started wondering about babies" (and simultaneously has taken to "tearing off low-hanging leaves or tall grass heads with a kind of wanton energy"), tells of viewing a birth with her medical school boyfriend while she was in college. The details she remembers and the horror she feels at the process are reiterated almost word for word by Esther Greenwood. Myra remembers walking in the hospital, past "blind, mushroom-colored embryos in the jars" and "four leather-skinned cadavers, black as burnt turkey." Esther, too, sees four cadavers with "leathery, purple-black skin," and big glass jars of fetuses. But what lingers with both women most strongly is the memory of the drugging of the patient and her subsequent forgetfulness of the pain of childbirth. Both blame the invention of the drug, which doesn't stop the pain, just induces later forgetfulness, a "twilight sleep," on the sinister intents of men. Both view men as acting for their own good without a concern for women's experience. Myra first describes her horror at the false security induced by the drug.

> Although erased from the mind's surface, the pain was there, somewhere, cut indelibly into one's quick—an empty, doorless, windowless corridor of pain. And then to be deceived by the waters of Lethe into coming back again, in all innocence, to conceive child after child! It was barbarous. It was a fraud dreamed up by men to continue the human race; reason enough for a woman to refuse childbearing altogether.

Esther later recalls the same scene, using even the image of "that long, blind, doorless and windowless corridor of pain" and noting that if women knew or remembered the pain they would forget about having children altogether. More than "Tongues of Stone," written in 1955, "Sweetie Pie and the Gutter Men," written in May of 1959, shows not just the same incident but Plath's increased thematic awareness. Myra has begun to focus on her discontent—more importantly, finding its source in the negative implications of her role as wife/mother. She finds herself having to bite back her views concerning being "just" a mother. She is depressed at the thought of joining the rest of women in this reproductive role and blames men for devising means to keep women unconscious of the pain involved. For Myra, this pain extends beyond the labor process and stretches into the rest of her potential lifetime as a mother. Myra's depression is presented less as a result of a personality defect and more as an understandable disgust with an undesired, unfulfilling expectation. She has begun to move into a clearer awareness of gender delineation and the politics of sexuality.

The fourth short story, "Johnny Panic and the Bible of Dreams," contains two shorter images rather than major events that move into *The Bell Jar*. The first is simply the description of a woman who enters the psychiatric clinic and whose dream the narrator seeks to record. The woman was brought to the Emergency Room because her tongue was stuck out and she couldn't return it to her mouth. This occurred during a party for her French-Canadian mother-in-law, whom she hated "worse than pigs." This same character appears equally briefly in the novel, in the state psychiatric ward, as Mrs. Tomolillo. Again, she has a hated French-Canadian mother-in-law, and again her symptom is the uncontrollable tongue which sticks out until it's swollen. The second image is more powerful, for it is crucial to both the story and the novel: the narrator's experience of electroshock treatment. In "Johnny Panic and the Bible of Dreams," the final scene is the administration of the shock treatment. In the misapplied shock, the narrator sees her first direct sight of Johnny Panic himself. He comes into view as she is "shaken like a leaf in the teeth of glory," while "the air crackled with blue-tongued lightning-haloed angels." The treatment is likewise described in *The Bell Jar*, when Dr. Gordon fails to properly administer the shock. "Then something bent down and took hold of me and shook me like the end of the world. Whee-ee-ee-ee-ee, it shrilled, through an air crackling with blue light."

What distinguishes this story from the three previously discussed is that for the first time the story is as strong a narrative as the novel. In part, this is because of the stylistic change to first-person. For the first time we have a conscious persona dealing with the experience of the breakdown. There is no additional narrator-filter to feeling and understanding the character. Further, "Johnny Panic and the Bible of Dreams" is a short story which contains a very central theme of Plath's, one which she is building up to in *The Bell Jar* and one which has appeared in other stories throughout the '50s not related to the breakdown: the need to validate the realm of imagination and possibility against the "real world," the world of limited and stereotyped roles. In "Johnny Panic," for the first time in the stories relating the story of her breakdown, Plath's narrator is not becoming aware of the conflict, she already understands it and has begun to act in response to it. She has taken up a battle that the other three narrators are just discovering might exist. It is this recognition and choice of action which thematically is the focus to almost all of Plath's fiction, even those stories which stand apart from the drafting of *The Bell Jar*.

Given the centrality of this theme, it is not totally coincidental that the two strongest characters in Plath's fiction, Esther Greenwood and the narrator of "Johnny Panic," are writers. Plath's major fictional characters, from Elizabeth Minton (in "Sunday at the Mintons'," 1952) forward, are all incipient artists. That is not to say that all, or most, are professional artists. Rather, they are, as so many characters in feminist fictions, engaged in creating themselves, reshaping the world around them to give significance to the actions and places in which they spiritually and actually reside. They come to see themselves as the creation of an imagination at odds with the culture and people around them. They are constantly striving to keep at bay the deadening, self-invalidating, oppressive sterility of the "real world," a world which devalues their experience and prohibits new patterns of thought and self awareness. Their true world is the realm of imagination, even if this imagination leads to socially defined madness. When not so extremely labeled, the characters are at least alienated from the technical, coldly rational world they exist in. They escape from this real world to the one of imagination, for none can accept a world which denies the power of fantasy, denies the right of each individual—regardless of gender—to be fully developed and fulfilled, denies (then electrically and chemically obliterates) the fears and thoughts of adults without replacing them with stronger beliefs and dreams.

Thematically, the feared death of the imagination runs throughout all of Plath's fiction in the decade preceding publication of *The Bell Jar*. Plath's characters reverse Hamlet's cry: they wish to dream, not sleep, much less just exist. As Plath explains in the "Cambridge Notes" excerpt from her journals:

> What I fear most, I think, is the death of the imagination. When the sky outside is merely pink, and the rooftops merely black; that photographic mind which paradoxically tells the truth, but the worthless truth, about the world. It is that synthesizing spirit, that "shaping" force, which prolifically sprouts and makes up its own worlds with more inventiveness than God which I desire. If I sit still and don't do anything, the world goes on beating like a slack drum, without meaning. We must be moving, working, making dreams to run toward; the poverty of life without dreams is too horrible to imagine; it is that kind of madness which is worst: the kind with fancies and hallucinations would be a Boschish relief.

The main characters in "Sunday at the Mintons'" (1952), "Superman and Paula Brown's New Snowsuit" (1955), "The Wishing Box" (1956),

"All the Dead Dears" (1956/57), "Stone Boy with Dolphin" (1957/58), and "Johnny Panic and the Bible of Dreams" (1958) all express a need and determination to foster and live in a world governed more by that "synthesizing spirit," that God-like personal inventiveness, than the social strictures of the people around them. For example, Elizabeth Minton's fanciful daydreams are continually interrupted by her brother Henry, a demanding but practical man. Elizabeth's image for their differences is summed in her imagined view of the interior of their minds. Henry's mind would be "flat and level, laid out with measured instruments in the broad, even sunlight. . . . The air would be thick with their accurate ticking." Conversely, her mind would be "a dark, warm room, with colored lights swinging and wavering . . . and pictures . . . [and] from somewhere sweetly coming, the sound of violins and bells." Clearly her preference (and the author's) is for the vague impressionist world of her mind.

Likewise, in "The Wishing Box," Agnes Higgins despairs of her loss of dreams. She can remember "her infinitely more creative childhood days," but she seems doomed to be unable to recapture them in the adult world in which she now lives. Suicide finally releases her from her empty reality to another world, "some far country unattainable to mortal men . . . [where she is] waltzing with the dark, red-caped prince of her early dreams." More importantly, Agnes' death is a triumph, not a defeat, for she *does* reenter the world of the imagination.

Similarly, in "Stone Boy with Dolphin" Dody Ventura longs for something to happen, for something to match the intensity of her dreams. Her dreams are peopled by visionaries:

> In her third-floor attic room she listened, catching the pitch of last shrieks: listened: to witches on the rack, to Joan of Arc crackling at the stake, to anonymous ladies flaring like torches in the rending metal of Rivera roadsters, to Zelda enlightened, burning behind the bars of her madness. What visions were to be had come under thumbscrews, not in the mortal comfort of a hot-water-bottle-cozy cot. Unwincing, in her minds' eye, she bared her flesh.

Although all the characters mentioned (witches, Joan of Arc, Zelda) are "mad," their madness is the "Bosch-ish relief" that Dody (and her creator) craves. This same craving is most graphically presented in "Johnny Panic and the Bible of Dreams," where the narrator's entire life's goal is to be the recorder of dreams, the treasurer of the imaginative world which both underlies and runs counter to the pragmatic world we recognize as "reality."

Plath's short stories show her development as a fiction writer. Stylistically and thematically they prefigure and serve as her apprenticeship for *The Bell Jar*. Without them as test grounds, *The Bell Jar* could not have been so rapidly produced, so strongly presented. After all the pre-tellings and thinking, in *The Bell Jar* Plath is able to move into her own narrative voice and pace. Her well-wrought and hard wrung apprenticeship yielded to a haunting powerful craftsmanship.

Chronology

1932   Sylvia Plath, the first child of Aurelia Schober and Otto Emil Plath, is born on October 27 in Boston.

1936   The Plath family moves to the seaside town of Winthrop, Massachusetts.

1940   Otto Emil Plath dies.

1942   The family moves to Wellesley, Massachusetts.

1942–50   Plath writes her first poems and short stories while attending public schools in Wellesley.

1950   Plath wins a scholarship to Smith College.

1953   Plath ventures to New York to work as a *Mademoiselle* guest editor for the summer. She attempts suicide later that year, but is discovered and hospitalized.

1954   Plath returns to Smith. She attends Harvard summer school on scholarship.

1955   Plath graduates from Smith. She travels to England to study at Cambridge University on a Fulbright fellowship.

1956   On June 16 Plath marries Ted Hughes.

1957   Accompanied by her husband, Plath returns to Smith College as a visiting professor.

1958   While residing in Boston, Plath audits Robert Lowell's poetry classes at Boston University and writes.

1959   Plath and Hughes visit Yaddo. They return to England to make their home in London.

1960   Plath's first child, Frieda Rebecca, is born on April 1. *The Colossus and Other Poems* is published in October.

1961   The family moves to Devon.

1962   On January 17 Plath's son, Nicholas Farrar, is born. Plath and Hughes separate in December; Plath and the children move to London.

1963   Under the pseudonym Victoria Lucas, Plath publishes *The Bell Jar* in January. On February 11 she commits suicide.

1965   *Ariel* is published.

1966   *The Bell Jar* is reprinted.

1971   Two more collections of Plath's poetry, *Crossing the Water* and *Winter Trees,* are published.

1975   *Letters Home* is published.

1977   Hughes compiles *Johnny Panic and the Bible of Dreams and Other Prose Writings* for publication.

Contributors

HAROLD BLOOM, Sterling Professor of the Humanities at Yale University, is the author of *The Anxiety of Influence, Poetry and Repression,* and many other volumes of literary criticism. His forthcoming study, *Freud: Transference and Authority,* attempts a full-scale reading of all of Freud's major writings. A MacArthur Prize Fellow, he is general editor of five series of literary criticism published by Chelsea House. During 1987–88, he served as Charles Eliot Norton Professor of Poetry at Harvard University.

IRVING HOWE is Distinguished Professor of English at Hunter College. His best-known book is *World of Our Fathers.* He is also known for his studies of Faulkner, Hardy, and Sherwood Anderson.

D. F. McKAY is Professor of English at the University of Western Ontario.

STAN SMITH is the author of *Inviolable Voice: History and Twentieth-Century Poetry* and *Rereading Literature: W. H. Auden.*

SANDRA M. GILBERT is Professor of English at Princeton University. She is coauthor with Susan Gubar of *The Madwoman in the Attic* and coeditor (also with Gubar) of *Shakespeare's Sisters: Feminist Essays on Women Poets* and *The Norton Anthology of Literature by Women.*

HUGH KENNER, Professor Emeritus of English at Johns Hopkins University, is the leading critic of the High Modernists (Pound, Eliot, Joyce) and of Beckett. His books include *The Pound Era, The Stoic Comedians, Dublin's Joyce,* and *Ulysses.*

J. D. McCLATCHY teaches creative writing at Princeton University. He is the author of three volumes of poetry, and the editor of *Anne Sexton: The Artist and Her Critics.*

MARY LYNN BROE is Associate Professor of English at the State University of New York at Binghamton. She is the author of *Protean Poetic: The Poetry of Sylvia Plath.*

TED HUGHES is Poet Laureate of England. His many volumes of poetry include *Lupercal, Woduo, Crow,* and *Gaudete,* his most recent collection. He has written several articles on Sylvia Plath.

LYNDA K. BUNDTZEN is Associate Professor of English at Williams College. She is the author of *Plath's Incarnations: Woman and the Creative Process.*

SUSAN VAN DYNE is Associate Professor of English at Smith College. She has written numerous articles on Sylvia Plath and other twentieth-century poets.

MELODY ZAJDEL is Assistant Professor of English at Montana State University and the author of several articles on modern and contemporary poetry.

Bibliography

Aird, Eileen. *Sylvia Plath: Her Life and Work*. Edinburgh: Oliver & Boyd, 1973.

———. "Variants in a Tape Recording of Fifteen Poems by Sylvia Plath." *Notes and Queries* 19 (1972): 59–61.

Aldrich, Elizabeth. "Sylvia Plath's 'The Eye-mote': An Analysis." *Harvard Advocate* 101 (May 1967): 4–7.

Alexander, Paul, ed. *Ariel Ascending: Writings about Sylvia Plath*. New York: Harper & Row, 1985.

Alvarez, A. "The Art of Suicide." *Partisan Review* 37 (1970): 339–58.

———. "Prologue: Sylvia Plath." In *The Savage God*. London: Weidenfeld & Nicolson, 1971.

Anderson, Lee. Interview with Sylvia Plath in the Lee Anderson Collection of Recorded Poets at the Yale Collection of Historical Sound Recordings, Yale University Library.

Annas, Pamela J. "The Self in the World: The Social Context of Sylvia Plath's Late Poems." *Women's Studies* 7 (1980): 171–83.

Axelrod, Stephen Gould. "The Mirror and the Shadow: Plath's Poetics of Self-Doubt." *Contemporary Literature* 26 (1985): 286–301.

Bagg, Robert. "The Rise of Lady Lazarus." *Mosaic* 2 (Summer 1969): 9–36.

Balitas, Vincent D. "On Becoming a Witch: A Reading of Sylvia Plath's 'Witch Burning.'" *Studies in the Humanities* 4 (February 1975): 27–30.

Ballif, Gene. "Facing the Worst: A View from Minerva's Buckler." *Parnassus: Poetry in Review* 5 (1976–77): 231–59.

Barnard, Caroline King. *Sylvia Plath*. Boston: Twayne, 1978.

Bedient, Calvin. "Oh, Plath!" *Parnassus* 12–13 (1985): 275–81.

Beirne, Daniel J. "Plath's 'Two Campers in Cloud Country.'" *Explicator* 42, no. 1 (Fall 1983): 61–62.

Berman, Jeffrey. "Sylvia Plath and the Art of Dying: Sylvia Plath (1932–1963)." *University of Hartford Studies in Literature* 10 (1978): 137–55.

Blodgett, E. D. "Sylvia Plath: Another View." *Modern Poetry Studies* 2 (1971): 97–106.

Boyers, Robert. "Sylvia Plath: The Trepanned Veteran." *Centennial Review* 13 (1969): 138–53.

Brink, Andrew. "Sylvia Plath and the Art of Redemption." *Alphabet* 15 (1968): 48–69.

Broe, Mary Lynn. *Protean Poetic: The Poetry of Sylvia Plath*. Columbia: University of Missouri Press, 1980.

Buell, Frederick. "Sylvia Plath's Traditionalism." *Boundary 2* 5 (1976–77): 195–211.

Bundtzen, Lynda K. *Plath's Incarnations: Woman and the Creative Process*. Ann Arbor: University of Michigan Press, 1983.

Burnham, Richard E. "Sylvia Plath's 'Lady Lazarus.'" *Contemporary Poetry* 1, no. 2 (1973): 42–46.

Butscher, Edward. *Sylvia Plath: Method and Madness*. New York: Seabury, 1976.

————, ed. *Sylvia Plath: The Woman and the Work*. New York: Dodd, Mead, 1977.

Caraher, Brian. "The Problematic of Body and Language in Sylvia Plath's 'Tulips.'" *Paunch* 42–43 (December 1975): 76–89.

Cooley, Peter. "Autism, Autoeroticism, Auto-da-fé: The Tragic Poetry of Sylvia Plath." *Hollins Critic* 10 (February 1973): 1–15.

Corrigan, Sylvia Robinson. "Sylvia Plath: A New Feminist Approach." *Aphra* 1 (Spring 1970): 16–23.

Coyle, Susan. "Images of Madness and Retrieval: An Exploration of Metaphor in *The Bell Jar*." *Studies in American Fiction* 12 (1984): 161–74.

Davis, Robin Reed. "The Honey Machine: Imagery Patterns in *Ariel*." *New Laurel Review* 1 (Spring 1972): 23–31.

————. "Now I Have Lost Myself: A Reading of Sylvia Plath's 'Tulips.'" *Paunch* 42–43 (December 1975): 97–104.

Davis, William V. "Sylvia Plath's 'Ariel.'" *Modern Poetry Studies* 3 (1972): 176–84.

Dickie, Margaret. "Sylvia Plath's Narrative Strategies." *Iowa Review* 13 (1982): 1–14.

Dobbs, Jeannine. "'Viciousness in the Kitchen': Sylvia Plath's Domestic Poetry." *Modern Language Studies* 7, no. 2 (1977): 11–25.

Donovan, Josephine. "Sexual Politics in Sylvia Plath's Short Stories." *Minnesota Review* 4 (1973): 150–57.

Dutta, Ujjal. "Poetry as Performance: A Reading of Sylvia Plath." *Literary Criterion* 16 (1981): 1–11.

Efron, Arthur. "Sylvia Plath's 'Tulips' and Literary Criticism." *Paunch* 42–43 (December 1975): 69–75.

————. "'Tulips': Text and Assumptions." *Paunch* 42–43 (December 1975): 110–22.

Eriksson, Pamela Dale. "Some Thoughts on Sylvia Plath." *UNISA English Studies* 10 (1972): 45–52.

Ferrier, Carole. "The Beekeeper and the Queen Bee." *Refractory Girl* (Spring 1973): 31–36.

Fraser, G.S. "A Hard Nut to Crack from Sylvia Plath." *Contemporary Poetry* 1, no. 1 (Spring 1973): 1–12.

Furomoto, Atsuko. "An Approach to the World of Sylvia Plath—Through the 'Mirrors'." *Studies in English Literature* (Japan) 58 (September 1981): 75–88.

Gilbert, Sandra M. "Teaching Plath's 'Daddy' to Speak to Undergraduates." *ADE Bulletin* 76 (Winter 1983): 38–42.

Gordon, Jan B. "'Who Is Sylvia?': The Art of Sylvia Plath." *Modern Poetry Studies* 1 (1970): 6–34.

Hardwick, Elizabeth. "On Sylvia Plath." *New York Review of Books*, 12 August 1971, 3–6.

Hardy, Barbara. "The Poetry of Sylvia Plath: Enlargement or Derangement?" In *The Survival of Poetry,* edited by Martin Dodsworth. London: Faber & Faber, 1970.

Holbrook, David. *Sylvia Plath: Poetry and Existence.* London: Athlone, 1976.

———. "Sylvia Plath and the Problem of Violence in Art." *Cambridge Review* 90 (1969): 249–50.

Hughes, Ted. "Introduction." In *Johnny Panic and the Bible of Dreams,* by Sylvia Plath. London: Faber & Faber, 1977.

———. "Sylvia Plath's *Crossing the Water:* Some Reflections." *Critical Quarterly* 13 (1971): 165–72.

———. "Winter Trees." *Poetry Book Society Bulletin* 70 (Autumn 1971).

Jones, A. R. "Necessity and Freedom: The Poetry of Robert Lowell, Sylvia Plath, and Anne Sexton." *Critical Quarterly* 7 (1965): 11–30.

Juhasz, Suzanne. *Naked and Fiery Forms: Modern American Poetry by Women—A New Tradition.* New York: Harper & Row, 1976.

Kamel, Rose. " 'A Self to Recover': Sylvia Plath's Bee Cycle Poems." *Modern Poetry Studies* 4 (1973): 304–18.

Kenner, Hugh. "Ariel—Pop Sincerity." *Triumph* 1 (September 1966): 33–34.

Kissick, Gary. "Plath: A Terrible Perfection." *Nation,* 16 September 1968, 245–47.

Kroll, Judith. *Chapters in a Mythology: The Poetry of Sylvia Plath.* New York: Harper & Row, 1976.

Lane, Gary. "Sylvia Plath's 'The Hanging Man': A Further Note." *Contemporary Poetry* 2 (Spring 1975): 40–43.

———. *Sylvia Plath: New Views on the Poetry.* Baltimore: Johns Hopkins University Press, 1979.

Libby, Anthony. "God's Lioness and the Priest of Aycorax: Plath and Hughes." *Contemporary Literature* 15 (1974): 386–405.

Lowell, Robert. "Foreword." In *Ariel.* New York: Harper & Row, 1966.

Lucie-Smith, Edward. "A Murderous Art." *Critical Quarterly* 6 (1964): 355–63.

Martin, Wendy. " 'God's Lioness'—Sylvia Plath, Her Prose and Poetry." *Women's Studies* 1 (1973): 191–98.

McClatchy, J. D. "Staring from Her Hood of Bone: Adjusting to Sylvia Plath." In *American Poetry since 1960,* edited by R. B. Shaw. London: Carcanet Press, 1973.

McClave, Heather. "Sylvia Plath: Troubled Bones." *New England Review* 2 (1980): 447–65.

Meissner, William. "The Opening of the Flower: The Revelation of Suffering in Sylvia Plath's 'Tulips.' " *Contemporary Poetry* 1, no. 1 (Spring 1973): 13–17.

———. "The Rise of the Angel: Life through Death in the Poetry of Sylvia Plath." *Massachusetts Studies in English* 3 (Fall 1971): 34–39.

Melander, Ingrid. *The Poetry of Sylvia Plath: A Study of Themes.* Stockholm: Almqvist & Wiksell, 1972.

———. " 'The Disquieting Muses': A Note on a Poem by Sylvia Plath." *Research Studies* 39 (1971): 53–54.

———. " 'Watercolour of Grantchester Meadows': An Early Poem by Sylvia Plath." *Moderna Språk* 65 (1971): 1–5.

Moramarco, Fred. " 'Burned-up Intensity': The Suicidal Poetry of Sylvia Plath." *Mosaic* 15, no. 1 (Winter 1982): 141–51.

Morris, Christopher. "Order and Chaos in Plath's 'The Colossus.' " *Concerning*

Poetry 15 (Fall 1982): 33–42.

Newman, Charles, ed. *The Art of Sylvia Plath: A Symposium*. Bloomington: Indiana University Press, 1970.

Oates, Joyce Carol. "The Death Throes of Romanticism: The Poems of Sylvia Plath." *Southern Review* 9 (1973): 501–22.

Oberg, Arthur. "Sylvia Plath and the New Decadence." *Chicago Review* 20 (1968): 66–73.

Oettle, Pamela. "Sylvia Plath's Last Poems." *Balcony* 3 (Spring 1965): 47–50.

O'Hara, J. D. "An American Dream Girl." *Washington Post Book World,* 11 April 1971, 3.

Ostriker, Alicia. "'Fact' As Style: The Americanization of Sylvia." *Language and Style* 1 (1968): 201–12.

Perloff, Marjorie. "Extremist Poetry: Some Versions of the Sylvia Plath Myth." *Journal of Modern Literature* 2 (1972): 581–88.

———. "On Sylvia Plath's 'Tulips.'" *Paunch* 42–43 (December 1975): 105–9.

———. "'A Ritual for Being Born Twice': Sylvia Plath's *The Bell Jar*." *Contemporary Literature* 13 (Autumn 1972): 507–22.

Pratt, Linda Ray. "'The Spirit of Blackness Is in Us. . . .'" *Prairie Schooner* 47 (1973): 87–90.

Roland, Laurin K. "Sylvia Plath's 'Lesbos': A Self Divided." *Concerning Poetry* 9 (1976): 61–65.

Romano, John. "Sylvia Plath Reconsidered." *Commentary* 57 (April 1974): 47–52.

Rosen, Lois. "Sylvia Plath's Poetry about Children: A New Perspective." *Modern Poetry Studies* 10 (1981): 98–115.

Rosenblatt, Jon. "'The Couriers.'" *Explicator* 34, no. 4 (December 1975): item 28.

———. "Sylvia Plath: The Drama of Initiation." *Twentieth Century Literature* 25 (1979): 21–36.

Rosenthal, M. L., and Sally M. Gall. "'Pure? What Does It Mean?' Notes on Sylvia Plath's Poetic Art." *American Poetry Review* (May–June 1978): 37–40.

Sanazaro, Leonard. "The Transfiguring Self: Sylvia Plath, a Reconsideration." *Centennial Review* 27 (Winter 1983): 62–74.

Simpson, Louis. "Black Banded with Yellow." In *A Revolution in Taste: Studies of Dylan Thomas, Allen Ginsberg, Sylvia Plath, and Robert Lowell*. New York: Macmillan, 1978.

Skei, Hans H. "Sylvia Plath's 'Lady Lazarus': An Interpretation." *Edda* 4 (1981): 233–44.

Smith, Pamela. "The Unitive Urge in the Poetry of Sylvia Plath." *New England Quarterly* 45 (1972): 323–39.

Smith, Stan. "Waist-Deep in History: Sylvia Plath." In *Inviolable Voice: History and Twentieth-Century Poetry*. Atlantic Highlands, N.J.: Humanities Press, 1982.

Spendal, R. J. "Sylvia Plath's 'Cut.'" *Modern Poetry Studies* 6 (1975): 128–34.

Stade, George. "Introduction." In *A Closer Look at Ariel: A Memory of Sylvia Plath,* by Nancy Hunter Steiner. New York: Harper's Magazine Press, 1973.

Stainton, Rita T. "Vision and Voice in Three Poems by Sylvia Plath." *Windless Orchard* 17 (Spring 1974): 31–36.

Sumner, Nan McCowan. "Sylvia Plath." *Research Studies* 38 (1970): 112–21.

Talbot, Norman. "Sisterhood Is Powerful: The Moon in Sylvia Plath's Poetry." *New Poetry* (Sydney) 21 (June 1973): 23–36.

Taylor, Andrew. "Sylvia Plath's Mirror and Beehive." *Meanjin* 33 (1974): 256–65.

Uroff, Margaret D. "Sylvia Plath on Motherhood." *Midwest Quarterly* 15 (1973–74): 70–90.

———. "Sylvia Plath's Narrative Strategies." *Iowa Review* (Spring 1982): 1–14.

———. *Sylvia Plath and Ted Hughes.* Urbana: University of Illinois Press, 1979.

Vendler, Helen. "Crossing the Water." *The New York Times Book Review,* 10 October 1971, 4, 48.

Wagner, Linda, ed. *Critical Essays on Sylvia Plath.* Boston: G. K. Hall, 1984.

Walsh, Thomas P., and Cameron Northouse. *Sylvia Plath and Anne Sexton: A Reference Guide.* Boston: G. K. Hall, 1974.

Willhelm, Albert E. "Sylvia Plath's 'Metaphors.' " *Notes on Contemporary Literature* 10 (1981): 8–9.

Wood, David. "Art as Transcendence in Sylvia Plath's *Ariel.*" *Kyushu American Literature* 24 (May 1982): 25–34.

Acknowledgments

"The Plath Celebration: A Partial Dissent" by Irving Howe from *The Critical Point of Literature and Culture* by Irving Howe, © 1973 by Irving Howe. Reprinted by permission.

"Aspects of Energy in the Poetry of Dylan Thomas and Sylvia Plath" by D. F. McKay from *The Critical Quarterly* 16, no. 1 (Spring 1974), © 1974 by C. B. Cox. Reprinted by permission of Manchester University Press and C. B. Cox.

"Attitudes Counterfeiting Life: The Irony of Artifice in Sylvia Plath's *The Bell Jar*" by Stan Smith from *The Critical Quarterly* 17, no. 3 (Autumn 1975), © 1975 by C. B. Cox. Reprinted by permission of Manchester University Press and C. B. Cox.

" 'A Fine White Flying Myth': Confessions of a Plath Addict" by Sandra M. Gilbert from *The Massachusetts Review* 14, no. 3 (Autumn 1978), © 1978 by The Massachusetts Review, Inc. Reprinted by permission.

"Sincerity Kills" by Hugh Kenner from *Sylvia Plath: New Views on the Poetry*, edited by Gary Lane, © 1979 by The Johns Hopkins University Press. Reprinted by permission of The Johns Hopkins University Press.

"Short Circuits and Folding Mirrors" by J. D. McClatchy from *Sylvia Plath: New Views on the Poetry*, edited by Gary Lane, © 1979 by The Johns Hopkins University Press. Reprinted by permission of The Johns Hopkins University Press.

"The Bee Sequence: 'But I Have a Self to Recover' " by Mary Lynn Broe from *Protean Poetic: The Poetry of Sylvia Plath* by Mary Lynn Broe, © by the Curators of the University of Missouri. Reprinted by permission of the University of Missouri Press.

"Sylvia Plath and Her Journals" by Ted Hughes from *Grand Street* 1, no. 3 (Spring 1982), © 1982 by Ted Hughes and Grand Street Publications, Inc. Reprinted by permission.

"Women in *The Bell Jar*: Two Allegories" (originally entitled "The Allegory of the Double Standard") by Lynda K. Bundtzen from *Plath's Incarnations: Women and the Creative Process* by Lynda K. Bundtzen, © 1983 by the University of Michigan Press. Reprinted by permission.

"Fueling the Phoenix Fire: The Manuscripts of Sylvia Plath's 'Lady Lazarus'" by Susan Van Dyke from *The Massachusetts Review* 24, no. 2 (Summer 1983), © by The Massachusetts Review, Inc. Reprinted by permission.

"Apprenticed in a Bible of Dreams: Sylvia Plath's Short Stories" by Melody Zajdel from *Critical Essays on Sylvia Plath*, edited by Linda W. Wagner, © 1984 by Linda W. Wagner. Reprinted by permission of Linda W. Wagner and the author. Originally published by G. K. Hall & Co.

Index

PS
3566
L27
Z914
1989

Sylvia Plath.

$26.95

DATE			
WITHDRAWN			

CARROLL COMMUNITY COLLEGE LMTS

0 0000 00907 1531

Library / Media Center
Carroll Community College
1601 Washington Road
Westminster, Maryland 21157

JUN   2 1993   BAKER & TAYLOR BOOKS